THE
CANNIBAL

by Mel Heimer

NOVELS

Penniless Blues
The Look of Eagles
West Wind
A Family Affair

NONFICTION

The World Ends at Hoboken
The Big Drag
Fabulous Bawd: The Story of Saratoga
The Girl in Murder Flat
Inside Racing
The Long Count
The Cannibal

IN COLLABORATION

The Rampant Refugee (with Kathleen Carlisle)
Champagne Cholly (with Eve Brown)
Pittsburgh Phil (with Frank Mastroly)

THE CANNIBAL

BY MEL HEIMER

Xanadu

British Library Cataloguing in Publication Data

Heimer, Mel (Melvin Leighton), 1915-1971
   The cannibal: the case of Albert Fish.
   1. United States. Paedophilia. Fish, Albert
   I. Title
   306.7'7
   ISBN   0-947761-59-4

Copyright ©1971 by Mel Heimer

First published in the United States of America
by Lyle Stuart, Inc. 1971

This edition published by Xanadu Publications Ltd
19 Cornwall Road, London N4 4PH

Printed and bound in Great Britain by
Billing & Sons Limited, Worcester WR2 5JU

Acknowledgments

Among the many who helped put together the story of Albert Fish, special thanks to Thomas Fracelle, chief assistant district attorney of Westchester County, New York; the Explorers Club; New York State Supreme Court Justice Elbert Gallagher; Attorney James Dempsey; Dr. Frederic Wertham; and Louise Metzger, librarian, and Joseph Miller, research specialist, at King Features Syndicate.

—M. H.

Mordre wol out, certeyn, it wol not faille.

—Chaucer, *The Prioress's Tale*

1.

THE DETECTIVE'S name was William King, and he had been in the room for a week now, waiting. Room Eleven.

Room Eleven, 200 East 52nd Street, just off Third Avenue, New York City.

Detective King was chain-smoking, which wasn't new. He had chain-smoked all week, waiting—and the man hadn't come. King had talked with his captain at the Missing Persons Bureau, John H. Ayres, and they had agreed that the man was more than a week overdue and it was beginning to look dubious.

There was a letter waiting for the man at 200 East 52nd Street, and it contained money. A check from his son, who was living and working at a Civilian Conservation Corps camp in North Carolina. The son sent the check every month, and every month the man came for it, no matter where he might have been. But this time he hadn't yet come for it, and it had arrived eight days before.

9

"Maybe he knows," Captain Ayres had said. "You never know how things like that get around. Maybe he's aware there's a policeman in his old room. Or simply somewhere in the house. You can't tell." King stubbed out another cigarette and, to himself, agreed. Maybe the man knew.

He was sitting in an old chair in Room Eleven, and then the doorbell rang and he got up automatically and went to the door of the room, opening it a trifle. He expected nothing. He had done the same thing dozens of times during his week's stakeout and there had been nothing.

He could hear snatches of the conversation but not enough to make any sense of it. Then he heard the click-clack of the landlady's shoes on the stairs. She was a stoutish bleached blonde who looked, well, like a landlady. She stopped at the door.

"That's him now," she said hurriedly. "I told him I was going to my room to get his check."

King nodded and let out his breath.

It had been worth waiting for. This much had been, anyway. Where it went from here was anybody's guess. He pulled his necktie up snug against his collar, opened the door, and went down the stairs.

The man in the foyer was a gray man. He looked in his sixties, maybe older, and he had a thin face, with sparse gray hair and a thin, straggly, gray mustache. He wore a black suit and carried a black hat and he stood almost sleepily, blankly, waiting. He barely looked up when Detective King came toward him. The policeman already had his hand on his billfold with the badge in it. He looked at the gray man.

"Are you Albert Fish?" he asked. The little, aging man stared at him a moment, seemingly indifferent, and then nodded.

"Yes."

King showed his credentials. "I'm taking you down to headquarters," he said. The reaction of the other was a strange one—strange at least to the detective, who knew how people behaved when they were taken into custody. They cried, they got angry, they became indignant; they showed emotion in a dozen different ways.

Albert Fish just looked at him for a moment, then nodded and went with the detective. He didn't seem to care. He fumbled around for a razor blade in a jacket pocket, but King easily, gently, took it from him.

EVEN IN THE late morning of a winter day, which this was, Center Street in downtown Manhattan is a quiet, almost remote place. It is some blocks removed from Wall Street and the financial hotbed, the last part of lower New York where there is any life during the day—and almost none at night—and even the stream of lawyers and traffic violators drifting into the official buildings is a trickly one. And this was 1934, late 1934, when there were fewer criminals, not nearly so many lawyers, and virtually no errant motorists. Police headquarters was a hushed place. Patrolmen, desk officers, plainclothesmen seemed to be lazing through the morning, girding themselves for the night, when the elements fuse in bigtown.

In a small interrogation room, Captain Ayres, Detective King, and a sergeant, J. L. Sheridan, asked questions of Albert Fish. Routine, where-were-you-born, what-do-you-do-for-a-living questions at first.

In another room, a couple of policemen went through Fish's old, leather-strapped suitcase. There wasn't much out of the ordinary in it. Old clothes—some clean, some not—soiled handkerchiefs, slippers, the usual. Only the clippings were offbeat. There was a handful of them, bound together, and they all dealt with Fritz Haarmann.

ALBERT FISH was not Fritz Haarmann. Haarmann was dead. And he was dead four thousand miles away, in Hanover, Germany.

A few years after Haarmann's story had finished, William Bolitho described him, in *Murder for Profit*: "The chief murderer. The worst man. The last of the human race."

Haarmann was born October 25, 1879, and by the time he had become a middle-aged man, Hanover had become like so much of the rest of Germany in the early twenties: a sinkhole in which, for example, there were by police estimates forty thousand homosexuals. It was a city of degeneracy, robbery, murder, rape, and not much in the way of morals. The Great War had pinched and bled Germany, and its people had not sprung back. In Hanover they were, many of them, a cut above the animals.

Haarmann was a pudgy, rosy-cheeked baby, born to a bad-tempered father who had quit his job as a locomotive stoker, and to a mother seven years older than her husband, a mother who had had Fritz as her sixth child and then become bedridden at forty-one. Of the other five children, three were girls who lost their virginity early, a fourth was a boy who went to reform school for a morals offense against a twelve-year-old girl, and the fifth was another boy who went against the grain and ultimately became a hard-working, respectable foreman.

Haarmann was not the usual child.

He loved to dress up as a girl, and he hated his irascible father. Today those symptoms are signposts to child psychiatrists. Then, in the late 1800's, they only made Fritz Haarmann an odd child. He was good-looking but there were layers of fat on him.

At seventeen, he committed several offenses against children; the official records say no more than that. He was committed to an asylum at Hildesheim, where one examining doctor said he was "incurably feeble-minded." Haarmann didn't stay long. He escaped to Switzerland, where he worked at different jobs for several years, and then he returned to Hanover and his family. But he had no luck in leading a normal life, whatever that is. There were endless rows with his father. There was an engagement that was broken, and a stillborn child. Finally, Fritz went into the army in Alsace and started what he said were the happiest years of his life. Officers said of him that he was a born soldier.

An illness, diagnosed as neurasthenia, cut short his army career—and then he spent a third of the next twenty years in prison. Petty theft, burglary, fraud, indecency. World War One came and went and Haarmann was in jail—for theft, this time—throughout it. When he got out, the "war to end all wars" was over and the Schieber Market was waiting for him.

The Schieber Market, a noisy, crowded, alive area opposite the railway station in Hanover, had a double life. It was a legitimate layout for the sale of foodstuffs, and it also was a headquarters, a wheeling-dealing point, for the sale of stolen and smuggled meat, bought by hungry Germans with no questions asked.

Fritz Haarmann sold meat to the under-the-counter dealers.

Haarmann then lived at Cellarstrasse 27 in Hanover's old quarter, a seamy Teutonic kind of Casbah. With him lived Hans Grans, who was a roughly handsome gigolo type in appearance but actually was Fritz's lover. Haarmann became known as a *gehamstertes fleish* or smuggled-meat vendor.

The meat was that of young men.

The first missing youth was Friedel Rothe, a seventeen-year-old who had come from out of town by train and had been picked up by Haarmann at the railway station and taken to Cellarstrasse 27. There were a couple of suspects, one of them Fritz Haarmann. The police searched Haarmann's lodgings but went away satisfied there was nothing there.

They didn't look closely enough. Even as they searched, Friedel Rothe's head was under a newspaper behind the kitchen stove.

There were roughly six hundred disappearances of boys and young men between the years 1918 and 1923, in the Hanover area, but the police had no real leads on them. After February, 1923, until late in 1924, they had direct leads, once their case was complete, on the disappearances of twenty-seven males, aged mostly fifteen to eighteen. The leads led straight to Fritz Haarmann.

At night, neighbors told authorities, you could hear the sounds of chopping in Haarmann's apartment, and he apparently made few attempts to conceal the noise. He was, after all, a meat dealer. Once he even gave some bones to a neighbor and urged her to make soup with them, but she told police later "they were so very white. After I made the soup, I became suspicious and threw it away."

In 1924 finally, many skulls were unearthed on ground near Haarmann's lodgings. When he was arrested, he tried to throw some of the blame on Hans Grans, and Grans petulantly threw it back at him. Fritz Haarmann was beheaded by the law.

IN THE interrogation room at Police Headquarters, the questioning of Albert Fish went on patiently, methodically. In the meantime, Sergeant G. R. Hamill had gone to an apartment house in West 15th Street. He asked for Edward Budd, Jr., and that man, now a twenty-four-year-old, went with Sergeant Hamill to headquarters.

When they arrived at Center Street, Captain Ayres was

told, and he rounded up four police department employees. Two were civilians, one was a captain, and the fourth a plainclothes lieutenant. The four of them all were past middle age, had gray hair, and were mustachioed. They were taken to the line-up room and there, with Albert Fish among them, were shuffled across the little stage, in an impromptu line-up, the lights glaring on them, the viewers in the darkness before them. Edward Budd took no time at all. In the semidarkness, he pointed his finger at Fish. "That's him," he said. "That's Frank Howard."

Captain Ayres nodded, had the four policemen and civilian employees sent back to their jobs, and then shepherded Albert Fish back to the interrogation room. A stenographer sat nearby to take notes. The questioning began again and, with the necessary technical items of detail out of the way, the questioners could get down to the solid part.

The mousy, mild-mannered Fish didn't balk at all. He even seemed eager. Almost pathetically eager.

"I saw Edward Budd's ad in the *World*," he said with obvious relish. "I get a lot of leads that way. So I called at the house and said my name was Frank Howard." He went on from there, the words tumbling out, incoherent sometimes but, for the most part, telling the story the police had thought they might hear. But there was even more to it than they had suspected. Albert Fish went on talking, and the police never had heard anything like it.

> Suffer little children to come unto me,
> and forbid them not; for such is the
> Kingdom of God.
>
> —Mark, X, 14

2.

EDWARD BUDD, SR., and his wife Delia lived in the West 15th Street apartment house on the edge of New York's Chelsea section, with their children, Edward, Jr., who was eighteen, Albert, George, Beatrice, and Grace, who was twelve and a student at a nearby public school. They made up a more or less ordinary New York family, with less than average means, God-fearing and all the rest. They were city people, and Manhattan was a way of life for them—except for young Edward. In May of 1928, summer was coming on and Edward wanted to get out of bigtown. He wanted it badly. Somewhere along the line he had inherited a distaste for the noise and dirt of the city. On Monday, May 21, he put an advertisement in the situations-wanted columns of the *World*: "Young man, 18 years old, wishes position in the country for the summer."

The elderly man came to the house on Wednesday, May 23. He was thin and brown-eyed and dressed conservatively, and he looked slightly seedy but quite respectable. "Good morning," he told Mrs. Budd, "I'm Frank Howard and I have a vegetable truck garden near Farmingdale, Long Island. Is it your son who wants work in the country this summer?"

Mrs. Budd called Edward, and the three of them sat in the living room of the small apartment on the spring day. It developed that Mr. Howard also had a half-dozen milk cows on his Long Island farm, and was the father of six children. "I'm a widower," he explained, going on to say that only one of his children was at the farm then, "so I certainly can use an extra hand."

They talked details. Mr. Howard said Edward would have room and board and twenty dollars a month during the summer. It was what the boy wanted to hear. "When do I start?" he asked, smiling happily. Howard said that he would be back in town either the following day or on Sunday to visit his sister, after which he would pick up Edward and drive him to Farmingdale.

"Come a little early," Mrs. Budd said graciously, "and have dinner with us." Howard thought that would be fine and said he would let her know which day it would be.

Mrs. Budd asked him who did the cooking for him. "Do you have a woman who works in the house?" she asked.

The old man shook his head apologetically. "*I* do it," he said, "but I don't like it. If you had a daughter about young Edward's age, I'd give her a job, too."

Grace Budd was too young, however. At twelve, a child couldn't get her public school working papers. That seemed too bad.

Howard did not come Thursday. He sent a wire, however, saying he would be there Sunday. And he was.

"NOW, EDWARD," Mrs. Budd said, "behave yourself."

17

"Yes, Mom."

"Work hard. Hard work never hurt anyone."

"Sure, Mom."

"And don't forget to brush your teeth after meals every day, do you understand?"

"Aw, Mom."

It was the morning of Sunday, May 27, and the young Budd's suitcase long had been packed and he was anxious to be off to the country. Mrs. Budd, a little sad because her eldest child would be gone for the entire summer, had set the table with the best dishes and had a chicken roasting in the oven.

When Frank Howard came, he was on time and he sat down at the dining room table with the Budds. It was the first time he had seen little Grace, a pretty brown-haired girl not yet quite slipped over into the beginnings of young womanhood.

She was just the right size.

Edward was a little too big.

The elderly gray man asked if he might say grace, and all bowed their heads. With great fervor, he asked a blessing on the house, the food, and all of them. When he had finished, he brought out a jar of cottage cheese from his pocket, an ordinary jar with no label on it, the sort of glass that in the old days a woman would have used to put up preserves. "This is from my farm," he said, giving the cottage cheese to Mrs. Budd, and he turned to the meal. He ate well and with obvious manners. There was apple pie for dessert and, as he toyed at it with his fork, he looked at Grace and smiled.

"I know of a party," he said, almost as if it were a secret between them. "I'll bet you'd like to go to one." She looked up at him, smiling, and beginning to become excited. Howard nodded and looked at the others, his face gentle and shining. "You see," he said, "kids never can pass up a party. Especially little girls."

It seemed that his sister was having a party that day for her daughter and a few of the daughter's girl friends—all of them in Grace's age range.

"I imagine it's a little unusual, and I wouldn't be offended if you said no," he said to the older Budds, "but it *will* be a nice party, I'm sure, and I think Grace would like it." He took out his pocket watch. "I think we could be up there shortly, spend a nice couple of hours at the party and be back at, say, four o'clock. Then Edward and I can head out to my farm at Farmingdale."

"I don't know," Mr. Budd said. "I don't know." Grace squirmed in her chair. "Oh, Daddy!" she said, and for awhile there was talk of the party, around the dining room table. At last the Budds said it seemed all right.

"Where does your sister live, Mr. Howard?" Budd asked.

"On Columbus Avenue near 137th Street. It won't take long to go there and come back."

To the party they went.

They left the 15th Street apartment building at twenty minutes after one, that spring Sunday. It was a lovely day. May in New York. May and October. There are no two finer months anywhere.

The Budds had overlooked one thing. Columbus Avenue reached only to 110th Street.

HAND IN HAND, the old man and the young girl walked across town a couple of blocks to Union Square, the big clearing of a few blocks in the neighborhood of 14th Street, hard by Klein's and Ohrbach's department stores, where the radicals demonstrated from time to time, and mounted police occasionally rode them down, prompting cries of "Cossacks!" On this Sunday early afternoon, however, the Square was quiet. Only drunks and lost, confused souls sprawled on the park benches, and the word for the day was peace.

They were headed for the 14th Street station of the IRT. "We'll go to Grand Central Terminal at 42nd Street," Howard/Fish told Grace, "and then take a *real* train to my sister's house that way."

Before they ducked down into the dinginess of the subway station, however, Fish stopped at a nearby newsstand. He nodded to the man inside the kiosk, passed a dime over to him, and was given a brown paper parcel that, a couple of hours before, he had asked the newsstand man to hold for him. The parcel was bound neatly and wasn't overlarge, but it seemed to be hefty as Fish took it, then turned and took Grace's hand again.

The train wasn't crowded. Side by side the two of them sat, looking like a proud grandfather out with his nicest little granddaughter. They reached Forty-second Street, got out and walked upstairs to the Grand Central Terminal where they boarded a Hudson Division train heading upstate. "Sit next to the window," Fish said to her. "You can see more there. It's a pretty ride." She did, and he took the aisle seat, putting his heavy brown paper parcel between them.

It *was* a pretty ride. On the Hudson Division of the then New York Central Railroad, you came out of the long tunnel area uptown, snaked around the edge of the dingy Harlem River for a bit, and then headed north along the eastern edge of the Hudson. To Grace the train seemed to be rolling along almost on top of the water. The river was slate-colored and, across the way, a quarter or three-eighths of a mile or so, the majestic Palisades reared, not yet filled with the greenery of summer but still giving little hints here and there of the warm-weather splendor to come. The train made frequent stops—Spuyten Duyvil, Riverdale, Ludlow, Yonkers—and finally at a station called Irvington in Westchester County. Fish took Grace's hand.

"Come," he said. "This is where we get off."

He led the way to the train vestibule, went down the stairs, stood on the platform, and held out his arms for Grace to hop off to him. For a moment, she held back, eyes wide. "Wait!" she exclaimed, and she pushed open the inner train door again and ran inside. She was back in a few seconds, struggling with the heavy parcel.

"Your package," she said. "You forgot your package!"

Fish stared a moment, then slowly took it from her. She clambered down the train steps and took his hand again. He nodded with his head at a street leading to a wooded area. "This way," he said. "My sister's house is just over there a little."

The house was a ramshackle, decaying old gray board structure, in the Greenburgh area adjacent to Irvington, with a faded blue sign on it saying "Wisteria Cottage." It was at the end of a street, somewhat removed from other houses, and behind it was only woods. It was the kind of place that kids liked to think of as haunted, and they played ghost games in it whenever there weren't winos or hoboes around, sleeping off jags or getting in out of the cold.

Fish pushed open the old door and they went into the musty rooms. "Why don't you go out back and pick some of the wild flowers?" he asked. "I'll see where my sister is." Grace was a little bewildered. No one seemed to be living there or to have lived there recently. But she *was* in the country, where the leaves were green now and the flowers were beginning to come up. She went out of the rear of the stale, creaky building and walked around, hunting for blossoms.

IN ONE OF the upstairs rooms, Fish got ready.

There were a warped round table and a couple of sagging chairs and Fish, first taking off his topcoat, removed all his clothes and put them on one of the chairs. Naked, scrawny,

21

old, and dead-white of flesh, he reached for the brown-paper package, which he had laid on the floor. *My implements of Hell,* he was to call them later. He opened the package and took them out: a butcher knife, long, thick and honed to the sharpest of edges; a small saw; and a cleaver.

He laid them out on the rickety table neatly. Then he went to the window and, standing just a little to one side so he would not be seen too clearly from the outside, he called to Grace Budd. She straightened up from the patches of weeds and flowers and came in through the back door, going upstairs. When she saw the nude old man, she stopped short and her eyes widened. Then she screamed.

"I'll call Mama!" Grace yelled, but that was as far as she got. Moving across the room more quickly than one would have thought an old man could, he reached her side and then, with his thin, bony hands sweating and twitching, he grabbed the girl by the throat and started to choke her.

She was only twelve and not all that big, but she fought more than he had expected. Fish held on to the thin throat and kept squeezing. Then he pushed, hauled her to the floor, and, as he watched her fading into unconsciousness, he put one of his thin knees onto her chest and shoved with that, to get all the breath out of her.

It was, Fish was to say later, "to get her out of her misery."

It took, maybe, five minutes. Then it was done and the old man leaned back, sweat running down his back and arms, and finally straightened up. Sunlight came in through the streaked windows, touching here and there on the body of the little girl. Fish's hands were fairly steady as he went to the table and took up the knife and cleaver.

Then he cut up the body as completely as a man in a meat market would split the torso of a steer into sections. He ended by cutting off the little girl's head. The dusty old room, flecked by sunlight, was bloody beyond imagination.

The ritual was only half over.

He took the lower part of Grace's body under one arm and the rest of her torso under the other. There were still other parts lying around, such as the arms. Knees bent from his burden, he went slowly over to a corner by the door of the room, dropped the pieces of body there, and opened the door against them so they were half-hidden.

The head, he wrapped in paper and carried through the area of the rear room. He pushed open the door tentatively, looking, but there was no one. Only the woods reared up behind the old house. His bare feet crunching on earth and stones, he carried the head to the outdoor toilet a few yards away and left it there.

He came back to the house and the inside room and looked at the other pieces of body. Then Fish took a part of a forearm and other small pieces and wrapped them in a bandanna handkerchief that was in a pocket of his jacket. He placed it on the table. Then he went to his topcoat and from it took a piece of absorbent cotton and a little bottle of cigarette lighter fluid. His hand still steady, but his eyes shiny-bright, the old man soaked the cotton in the fluid. Then he bent over and put the wet cotton firmly into his anus. He reached down to the topcoat again and took out some kitchen matches.

Bending over slightly, he struck one of the matches on the rough, worn surface of the table, reached around . . . and lighted the cotton.

It flared up quickly and there was the sudden whip of pain along his buttocks, and the smell of flesh burning. The old man began to dance—or jump around, rather; it was too incoherent a movement, too ragged a whirling around, to be called a dance. He began to yell, like an Indian in a war dance.

23

Finally, orgasm racked the absurd old body.

When it was done, Fish leaned heavily against the round table with his eyes closed. When he opened them, the parts of the body still were there and Fish could not remember what it had been. He felt it must have been a boy. Yes, a boy; that was it.

WHEN HE had dressed himself again, he picked up the bandanna with the piece of forearm in it and slowly went out the front door. He walked away from Wisteria Cottage without looking back and started out through streets, path, and brush to the train station.

The next morning, home, Fish went to a grocery, where he bought three pounds of potatoes, two pounds of onions, some carrots, and a sheaf of parsley. There was no need for salt and pepper; he had them. At a dairy he stopped and got a quart of milk.

He then went back to his rooms, took an old soot-blackened stew pot, removed the piece of forearm from the bandanna and, with his cleaver, chopped it into four parts. He dropped them into the pot, added some vegetables, a quart of water, and a bouillon cube, made a fire under the stew pot, and sat back on the floor, cross-legged, and watched it boil.

Then he ate his meal.

He practiced cannibalism for some days. Every couple of days he went up to Wisteria Cottage and got some more pieces of Grace Budd's body. He took them home and cooked them, sometimes with the remainder of the vegetables, sometimes with strips of bacon. And he ate them.

He ate them during the days, and at night, lying on his bed, he thought about what he had done and there were more orgasms. To Albert Fish it was "wonderful," lying there in the dark of the spring evenings and thinking of the scene in the house. The little body lying there. The terrible, marvelous pain he had felt. Pain was so magnificent (if only, as he said incongruously later, "it didn't hurt so much").

After nine days, he took the remaining parts of Grace Budd's body and threw them over an old stone retaining wall to the rear of Wisteria Cottage.

The episode was done.

YANK: Sure! Lock me up! Put me in
a cage! Dat's de on'y answer
yuh know. G'wan, lock me
up!
POLICEMAN: What you been
doin'?
YANK: Enough to gimme life for! I
was born, see? Sure, dat's de
charge. Write it in de blotter.
I was born, get me?

—Eugene O'Neill, *The Hairy Ape*

3.

THE GRACE BUDD incident. It was just
that part of the iceberg above the water.

Something or somebody, over the years, must have taken
the small boy who played in the streets of Washington,
D.C., ultimately to the pebbly path leading to Wisteria Cottage.

Or was the path always there from the start?

To begin with, his name actually was Hamilton Fish, the
"Hamilton" coming from what he said was a distant ancestor, Hamilton Fish, who during President Grant's two terms
of office had been the secretary of state and was called "the
pillar of the Administration." Long years later there was to

be another well-known American of the same name, a congressman who brought down on himself the scorn of President Franklin D. Roosevelt when, during World War Two, FDR used his scathing isolationist-accusing phrase: "Martin, Barton, and Fish." The first Hamilton Fish, the secretary of state, had been named Hamilton by a father who had been a close friend and then executor of the estate of Alexander Hamilton.

The Fish family in Washington, D.C., then, was a respectable one, although only of moderate means. Albert Howard Fish was born in 1870, and the way ahead at the time looked fair enough, except that, when he was five, his father died and his mother had to go to work. She placed Albert in an orphanage.

What roots there might have been, went quickly. Young Albert became almost overnight a stammering, nervous, upset child. Until he was eleven, he was a bed-wetter, and it took him until he was fifteen to be graduated from the eighth grade. The school was at the orphanage and, because it upset him to be called "Ham" or "Ham and Eggs," he changed his name to Albert. He ran away regularly; he said later that it seemed as if he did so every Saturday.

He had only inklings then of there being more to the Fish family than just the surface facts.

Over a period of two generations, *seven* persons in the family either suffered from psychoses or had severely psychopathic personalities. A younger brother of Albert's was feeble-minded from the start and died of hydrocephalus. Fish's mother was looked on by neighbors and even by friends as a queer one, who said frequently that she saw and heard "things" on the street. An uncle on his father's side had a "religious psychosis" and died in a state hospital. An aunt on his father's side was looked on as "completely crazy," in Fish's later words. Still another brother was a

27

chronic alcoholic, and a sister had "some sort of mental affliction." His father had been married before he wed Albert's mother and from that pairing came a half brother who died in a state institution.

Where Fish's strange—career?—began, and when, no one was able to pinpoint directly. Most estimates made it about the turn of the century, giving him more or less thirty years to do what it was he felt he had to do.

When he got through school at the orphanage, he went to work, as poor children did then. First at a grocery store and later as a house painter's apprentice. If he had any trade for the rest of his life, it was painting. Along with decorating and odd jobs, that was what he did chiefly for a living from then on.

He was twenty-eight when he married.

The girl was nineteen and, with her, Fish had six children. Later there were five grandchildren. Long after, his wife said of him that "he was crazy," but she remained married to him for nearly twenty years. Then she left. She eloped with a man who had boarded at their house, "sold everything in the house," according to Fish, and left the children behind. The youngest was then three.

It seems almost unimaginable in the light of the years that led to 1928, but he appears to have been a careful, faithful, and conscientious father. His children agreed on that and, as he said, he "acted as both father and mother to them." Not that there weren't other mothers. Fish "married" three times more—none of the marriages valid, naturally, since he never had been divorced.

MANY PSYCHIATRISTS were to examine, probe, and dissect Fish and his habits, his twisted mind—but because of the way his mind so often drifted into strange and unrelated channels, they could not say exactly whether he was born as

28

he was, which was entirely possible with the mental aberrations within his family, or became that way because of circumstance.

This much the psychiatrists knew. When he was five, there was a woman teacher who would pull down the trousers or pull up the dresses of children and spank them on their bare buttocks. Most of them had the natural reaction: It hurt, and they cried. Albert Howard Fish liked it.

He liked being spanked, and he liked seeing others spanked.

"I always had a desire to inflict pain on others and to have others inflict pain on me," Fish said. "I always seemed to enjoy everything that hurt. The desire to inflict pain, that is all that is uppermost." Well . . . a "normal" perversion. The masochist, the sadist—they are not that much of a rarity in the world of civilization.

If that were all, Fish really would not have been so much apart from his fellows.

When he was arrested and examined, physicians were startled at one discovery in the midst of so many other macabre items: X-rays of his body showed twenty-nine needles in him, twenty-seven of them in the pelvic region. Some of them were the huge needles that sailing people use to repair canvas. They were of all sizes, and the eyes of many of them were still clear under the X-ray. Many had been in his body a long time; they were eroded and it was estimated conservatively that it would have taken at least seven years for them to reach that stage. Some were mere bits of steel remaining. They were in perilous places. Some were just above and beside the transverse and descending colon, some around the rectum, some quite near the bladder.

A son said he had found needles hidden away in a book his father had at home. The book was a collection of Edgar Allan Poe's stories; the needles were hidden at the start of the tale, "The Narrative of A. Gordon Pym."

29

There was no doubt, the medical men said, that the needles had been inserted through the skin rather than swallowed, and Fish confirmed this. He said he had stuck needles into his body for many years, near his genitals. At first he had stuck them in and then pulled them out again, but some went in so far he couldn't remove them. "I put them up under the spine," Fish said. "I did put one in the scrotum, too, but I couldn't stand the pain."

And he expanded his habit of putting needles into bodies —especially into the bodies of children.

It was hard to get Fish to give a really satisfactory explanation. He once gave five conflicting explanations to a psychiatrist: (1) he did it to relieve the pain from a hernia, (2) he got "a sexual kick out of it," (3) he was punishing himself for what he had done to others, (4) "voices told me to purge myself of sin by self-torture; that's what induced me to put them in," and (5) he thought he might kill himself by perforating his intestines.

FISH'S FANTASIES and his actions, it was to develop, swirled around and went in a dozen or more directions.

He was always on the move. Over a period of years, he lived or traveled through twenty-three states, from New York to Montana. Once settled into a city or town, he had the habit of writing obscene letters. Not just at random. He would buy cheap magazines, with personal columns for the lovelorn (or would-be lovelorn) in them, or he would get names from matrimonial agencies. His obscene letters were not, on the whole, as incoherent as his life or behavior. They were to the point. He offered the letter-receivers his suggestions on what he wanted to do with or to them and have done to himself. He would write that he wanted to find a woman who would whip boys for and with him.

There was a woman who had advertised for elderly people who needed convalescent care. Fish wrote to her and, when she answered, went to see her. "He looked like an innocent man," the woman told authorities later, "but he had a rope or clothesline in a piece of wrapping paper and he said he wanted to be beaten with it. When he departed, he left the rope." She complained to the advertising agency involved and was told that it didn't see anything about which to complain.

Children were Fish's special prey.

He used his work as a now-and-then house painter to advantage to carry out his plans. Working frequently in public buildings, which would give him an excuse for investigating cellars, basements, and occasionally attics, he wore only overalls—nothing else except shoes and socks—particularly in warm weather. His reasoning was simple. When he had lured a child to a basement, he could be undressed in a couple of seconds. And, too, possible witnesses to his comings and goings would never have seen him in his ordinary street clothes.

What he would do was to bribe the children with small amounts of money or, more infrequently, just talk to them for a little and then forcibly push them into the cellar or wherever he had planned. Then he would . . . attack them. In many ways. "Fish," psychiatrist Fredric Wertham said, "was a polymorph perverse adult. There was no known perversion that he did not practice and practice frequently. I summarized them . . . eighteen perversions or paraphilias."

He hunted Negro children particularly. He found that police and other law-enforcement officials didn't go to as much trouble if it was a colored child abused or missing. In one town, Fish paid a little black girl a semi-regular salary of five dollars—to bring him little black boys.

How many? "At least a hundred," he admitted calmly later, but there never was a way of checking whether this

31

was many times short of the actual figure. Certainly, a hundred seems conservative. Now and then he would be particularly brutal, especially when he attempted to castrate the small boys. A year after the Budd murder, "I had a boy of thirteen. On a Sunday afternoon I was leading him away from home with the purpose to kill him and cut him up. I would have hit him on the head and then got the implements and cut what I wanted and then leave the rest out there. A number of automobiles came along while I was still looking for the proper place. If it hadn't been for the passing automobiles, I would have killed him."

He had intended, he said, to kill or castrate Edward Budd, Jr., but he found the boy too big and, for his bizarre taste, unattractive.

After he *had* been more brutal than usual, he packed up and left the area where he had been. He never went back to the same place; he was on the move for endless years, changing his address as other men change shirts, "and I have had children in every state." Sometimes he lost jobs "because things about these children came out." Then he moved on.

When it was all over, after the detective had waited for him in Room Eleven, Fish could remember the names of children he had attacked or killed, but the places where the outrages had occurred were misty to him. He was particularly clear about the details of an episode with a ten-year-old black boy named Noonan—one of the little Negroes brought to him by the little girl for five dollars a week. Fish said he gave Noonan some candy, told him of a party he knew about, took him to an unoccupied house—where he had just finished a painting job—and strangled the child. Using his "implements of Hell," he cut up the body, cooked part of Noonan's arm and then, noting that the boy had defecated while dying—which happens often in humans—also ate the feces with the rest of his dinner. It was, he remembered, the first time he had engaged in coprophagia (the eating of human waste).

IT WAS WHEN Fish was in his mid-fifties that the warping of his mind made a bend in another direction: religion.

He always had been extremely interested in the subject, but now he began to dwell on the need for "purging" himself, for suffering physically and making others suffer . . . and for human sacrifice. Hallucinations, delusions, and visions began to come. Occasionally he felt he *was* God and there was the urge to sacrifice one of his own sons, as Jesus was sacrificed. Or he identified with Abraham, who offered his son Isaac as a sacrifice. He thought he saw Jesus and angels. All these delusions were cloudy and uncertain to him, but he felt he heard the words "stripes," "rewardeth," and "delighteth." Fish fitted the words to Biblical passages: "Stripes means to lash them, you know. I could hear words spoken, and of course a great deal I have read. I could put the words together and see what they meant. Then I made up the rest from what I'd read."

In his own unreal world then, Albert Fish became the dark messenger of God.

He spoke in words such as: "Happy is he that taketh Thy little ones and dasheth their heads against the stones" and "Blessed is the man who correcteth his son in whom he delighteth with stripes, for great shall be his reward." More and more he turned to small children; he would bind, beat, castrate, and kill them. Sometimes he would gag them, when he had to for safety's sake, but mostly he liked to hear their cries.

One wonders how this man could go along year after year, go along the way he did, and not be caught. Well, he *was* caught. There were at least eight arrests, including six in 1930 alone, the disposition of three of which is not known. The charges included grand larceny (he embezzled money while working in a store), violation of parole, sending obscene letters, and so on. And to add to the eight specific arrests, there were innumerable times when he was picked up by police and held for questioning about having impaired the morals of minors.

Nothing stuck. No serious charge was proved. He did sixteen months in jail for the grand larceny charge, twenty-five days for an obscene-letter count, short periods for parole violations. It was frightening, thoroughly frightening, the way Albert Fish passed through authorities' hands like so much quicksilver.

Two and a half years after the Grace Budd affair, he was institutionalized in a psychiatric hospital for the first time, after his daughter had said he showed signs of mental disturbance. At that time, a nurse remembered seeing him kneeling in the bathtub, praying—yet he was freed as "not insane; psychopathic personality; sexual type." A federal court judge gave him six months' probation.

In the summer of 1931, he was arrested while working as a handy man in a hotel near a boarding school, the proprietor of which had complained to police about obscene letters. When his room was searched, a stick-and-leather cat o' nine tails was found, and he admitted freely to the police that he used it to whip himself. The psychiatrists were called in, and Fish's case was diagnosed as "sadism." That was all. He stayed two weeks at a hospital, where the nurses said he was "very restless" and "confused," but there was only one psychiatric examination. The report ended with these three words: *quiet, cooperative, oriented.*

"I am not insane," Albert Fish said later. "I am just queer. I don't understand it myself."

> You cannot understand me. No one
> can understand me.
>
> —Peter Kuerten, German mass
> murderer, to his judge

4.

ON ANY GIVEN night, New York City's Police Headquarters would be busy and bustling, naturally. Bigtown's crime rate might not be the highest in the nation but there are so many people there. What would be a month's haul of wrongdoers in, say, St. Louis, might be a night's work in the five sprawling boroughs of New York.

This night was a bit different, though. Little knots of the curious gathered outside headquarters. The disappearance of Grace Budd had occurred long ago but not long enough to erase it from memory. There was just the chance, for the curious, of seeing the kidnaper. Policemen on duty at headquarters found excuses to try to get a glimpse of Albert Fish, hanging about in corridors in the hope he would be coming in or out of a room. Newspaper reporters began to trickle into the big downtown building, and then the trickle became almost a torrent. Phones rang and shoes shuffled. There was yelling in the halls, and clerks and detectives moving this way and that briskly. Potential witnesses arrived, to identify the fugitive if they could. Headquarters was alive with movement.

In the interrogation room, the old man—he's only in his sixties, some elderly souls read in the papers indignantly; that's not *old;* but Fish looked old—seemed to tell his story with relish . . . and almost delight. Captain Ayres, aided now by Captain Stein, Detective King, and Deputy Chief Inspector John J. Ryan, put the questions to him patiently and in low key. They were professionals at work. As he came near the end of his story, Fish looked at the four of them with his disarming, gentle smile.

"I'm glad I told everything," he said. "It makes my conscience feel better."

Edward Budd, he said, had advertised in *The World* that he wanted summer work in the country. The advertisement almost jumped out of print, it seemed to Fish. He made up his mind. On a May day in 1928, he went to the Budd apartment house, an inexpensive lower-middle-class one with a little walk leading out to the sidewalk and a gate therein. Edward and his brothers and sisters were here and there around the house and outside it and Fish spoke to Edward at length.

"Actually," Mrs. Budd told Fish, "there are two of them who want summer jobs in the country, Edward and his friend Billy Korner. Fish nodded. "Two boys," he said calmly, "would suit my purpose better than one." Then he left, saying he would try to return the next day or the following Sunday.

He didn't come back the next day, though. There were plans to be made, things to be thought out, preparations to be completed. Instead, Fish went to a Western Union office at 104th Street and Third Avenue and sent a telegram to Mrs. Budd. He was, he explained in the wire, going to be detained in New Jersey buying a cow, and would arrive the following Sunday around noontime.

Before Sunday came the old man stopped at a pawn shop at 74th Street and Second Avenue in the Yorkville section of Manhattan. There, with no particular questions asked of him, he bought a cleaver, saw, and butcher knife. When he got them home, he wrapped them in a seven-by-four-foot tarpaulin with heavy brown paper outside of it and then, on Sunday, he took the subway downtown. At 14th Street near Union Square, only a few blocks from the Budd home, he asked a news dealer with a stand if he would mind his package for him.

Then, in his ill-fitting but reasonably presentable clothes, he turned and walked over to the apartment.

FOR FIFTEEN years, Edward Budd had been a porter in the Equitable Building on lower Broadway. Nobody looks at porters twice; not really. Now he was middle-aged, with a glass eye and a cataract on his good eye, a man not broken by the system, only worn out by it, because he never had reached any place in it from which he *could* have been broken. In the tiny, cluttered apartment on the fifth floor of the West 24th Street apartment building—they had moved since the tragedy of Grace's disappearance—he sat in the center of the small living room and tried to answer all of the reporters' questions at once. Yes, that appears to be the man, he said as they showed him pictures. Yes, he remembered well the Sunday that Albert Fish came to dinner and went away with his daughter. Budd's children—Edward, Jr., now twenty-four; Albert, twenty; George, nineteen; and Beatrice, eleven—sat around their father in a semicircle.

"I remember that when he came," Budd said, "he had a hat with a silk lining that must have cost ten dollars. His shoes were shined bright and he wore a wing collar on his shirt." The reporters scribbled. "I know that after we ate, he gave Edward and Willie Korner two dollars to go to the movies and they set out, taking Albert with them."

And what about when Fish asked if he could take Grace to the party? What about that?

"It seemed all right. He looked like a decent man. Grace, she was dressed in her confirmation dress, cut down like, and fixed up for regular days. She looked real sweet with her gray coat and hat. When he said she should come to the party with him, she was real happy. We didn't see anything wrong. We said she should go, and come home early."

Budd shook his head slowly, and his children seemed to edge in a little toward him, as if protectively. "We never did see her again," he said.

The questions came in bunches, reporters talking over one another, and Budd tried to be patient. He smiled ruefully. "They got this much stuff about us down at police headquarters," he said, holding his hands apart about a foot and a half, "a lot of them from cranks. Some of them from honest people. My wife, she says all the pictures look like that man. But it never is."

Stout, florid, jaw slightly undershot, Delia Budd sat apart in the next room, the kitchen. She had a cup of tea on the kitchen table by her, and one of the tabloids, which had been able to slip the story of the arrest into one of its early editions, was spread out. When reporters started questioning her she had nothing to say—except once, as she pointed to the picture in the newspaper of the kindly-looking old man.

"That's him," she said. "That's the dirty bum. I wish I had him here, so I could get my hands on him."

IT WAS Thursday, December 13, 1934, late in the afternoon, and Fish had told his story. Or as much as he felt like telling at the moment. From time to time he would add bits and pieces to it and then, when the psychiatrists trooped up to jail in Westchester to see him, he would really cut loose with big chunks of it. But this was all for the moment. Captain Stein and Detective King bundled him into an automobile, and in the cold gray December twilight they headed north for the neighboring county, specifically the town of Greenburgh and even more specifically, Wisteria Cottage in the Worthington Woods section.

They drove up the gentle incline to the cottage, which really was a small two-story house with a verandah around two sides of it, some distance back from a mountain road leading from the Saw Mill River Parkway to East Irvington. Westchester officials met the New York authorities there and, slowly but with obvious enthusiasm, Fish took them around the grounds.

The house still was deserted, still ramshackle, still dirty and smelling from years of disuse and misuse. The old man took them upstairs to the second floor and showed them the room where it had happened. He looked out the window thoughtfully. "Then when I came back to the house," he remembered, "I made a bundle of everything and threw the bundle out that window over there."

They went downstairs again, and he showed them where he had thrown the bundle over a stone wall. When he finally had ended his macabre Cook's tour and they still stood around in the chill suburban night, the Greenburgh police and the New York State troopers got busy with tools, flares, and searchlights and began digging and hunting. It wasn't too long before a crowd of several hundred persons had gathered—although much greater crowds would come by in the several days that followed. These were mostly residents of the area, attracted by the commotion and flares, along with a few townspeople from Greenburgh who had heard of what was going on.

The tools—the instruments of Hell—weren't to be found immediately. But there was one important find, the only one of the night. The troopers came up with the skull of a child. Quite conceivably, according to superficial diagnosis, the skull of a female twelve-year-old child, although there would be tests and more tests before anyone could say for certain.

THE POLICE do not always move with the speed of light in this sort of thing, but back at headquarters they were managing to put together at least a small dossier on Albert Howard Fish.

In his statements in the interrogation room, he had said he had been arrested once, far back in 1902, on a charge of burglary in Riverhead, Long Island. That, Fish said, was the extent to which he had been involved with the law. It wasn't quite so. A preliminary check disclosed a rather considerable police record—and the almost frightening fact that, within twelve weeks of the kidnaping of Grace Budd, the old man had been in the hands of the New York City police no less than three times. And had not been given a prison term on any of those occasions.

The record showed that Fish first had been arrested in 1903 in Suffolk County, Long Island (undoubtedly the 1902 case to which he had referred) and had been sentenced to from a year and a month to two years and two months in Sing Sing on a charge of grand larceny.

On July 21, 1928—Grace Budd's anemic little body hadn't truly decomposed yet, in its bits and pieces behind the Greenburgh cottage—Fish was arrested in Brooklyn on a grand larceny charge. A month later, on August 22, he was arrested in Manhattan on a charge of petty larceny. Each of these was discharged. And again on August 22, he was rearrested in the Bronx on a petty larceny charge. Suspended sentence.

40

There was a gap of nearly two years then. On May 2, 1930, Fish was arrested in Newark, New Jersey, on a vagrancy charge, but there was no immediate record of the case's disposition. In the fall of that year, late in September, he again was picked up in New Jersey, in Montclair this time, on a petty larceny charge, and received another suspended sentence. And finally in 1930, on December 15, he was arrested by federal authorities for sending indecent literature through the mails, and again there was no immediately known disposition.

LEAVING THE local police digging and fanning out their searchlights, the New York police and Fish returned to bigtown. The old man was taken to a cell in the detention pen at police headquarters—he was to be arraigned the following day in Jefferson Market police court on charges of abduction and homicide, although already it appeared as if any murder trial would be a Westchester affair—but he had one more ordeal to go through. It really didn't seem to bother him. At midnight, Edward Budd and Willie Korner, now young men in their early twenties, came to the cell and looked in at him. Mr. Budd was with them. Edward, who already had identified Fish, peered at the old man.

"Yes," he said, "that's him." Korner nodded in agreement. "Yes," he said, "that's the man that took Gracie away." Fish looked at him pleasantly. "Yes," he agreed, "that's the boy that was with Edward Budd."

Edward started yelling and reviling the old man, his face red with anger, and his father stepped up to Fish. "Don't you know me?" he asked. Fish looked at him closely and then smiled in recognition. "Yes," he said, "you are Mr. Budd." Budd sagged.

"And you," he said, "are the man who took my girl away to a party."

41

Up in Westchester they still were searching, into the small hours of the new day. In his cell, with belt, necktie, and shoestrings removed, Fish slept.

The sun came up and it was Friday, December 14, and the city was not too caught up in the eye of the still-present depression to turn its attention to the Grace Budd case and be genuinely shocked.

From what New Yorkers and indeed Americans across the country read, there seemed little doubt that Fish had accomplished the kidnap-murder—and to people everywhere, he was a new kind of criminal, a kind they could not understand.

America was not too long out of the twenties. Murder was realized with pistol or submachine gun fired from a long black car rolling through the streets. The country's assassins were simpler folk, plain old hoods who rubbed out one another. Readers looked at the pictures of the little gray man, seemingly so kind and harmless, and tried to fit the words to the photographs, but it was a little too much. They hadn't seen a one such as this before. The dailies still were calling themselves "home newspapers," and they sheltered subscribers from four-letter words and indelicate subjects. The full significance of what Fish had done was not reported totally . . . even so, there was a chance to get a pretty reasonable idea of it. But America read and did not understand. Fish was incomprehensible.

Around Wisteria Cottage in Greenburgh, the police continued their search. This time bones were found here and there, until there were enough to make a tidy little boxful. Dr. Amos O. Squire, the Westchester County Medical Examiner, made a cursory examination of them and said there was no doubt they were those of a child, quite probably in the neighborhood of twelve years old.

Four shoes were dug up. Three of them were just shoes,

thrown away by adults as if onto a dumping ground. The fourth was a little girl's. Another bone, some ten inches long, was discovered under the basement floor but it was decided that it was an animal's. Among the officials at the scene was Dr. Gilbert Daldorf, a pathologist at Grasslands Hospital in Valhalla, and it was he who found stains on the baseboard in the second-floor room and on part of the floor. The boards were hacked and ripped out from the building to be analyzed.

The saw and the cleaver were found, rust-covered, under leaves, with mold on them, although there still was no sign of the butcher knife. A Greenburgh truck driver named Jerry Real came forward and told police he had been at the scene some two years before, had seen and picked up the cleaver, found its handle rotted, and had thrown it away again into the underbrush. Near the cleaver, some white pearl-like beads were found. They apparently had been from a rosary Grace Budd had worn around her wrist.

Newsmen, digging around, came up with Mrs. Anna Straube of Astoria, Queens—Fish's former wife and the mother of his six children. She had, she said, divorced him twenty years before and since had married John Straube, by whom she had had three more children. She came to police headquarters after a while and proved to be a short, gray-haired, pleasant-looking woman.

Her comment to the press was to the point: "The old skunk. I knew something like this would happen sooner or later."

Another visitor to headquarters was Fish's oldest child, Albert, Jr., thirty-five, who, like his father, was a house painter by trade. He said that until two months before, his father had been superintendent of three sixteen-room apartment houses on Amsterdam Avenue in uptown Manhattan and that he, Albert, Jr., had worked for the old man as a painter.

43

There was nothing complicated about the younger Albert—he was a relatively simple man—but there was bewilderment and confusion. "Sometimes," he said a little uncertainly, "he used to scream out in the night in great fear. The tenants complained about him because he was so lazy and shiftless and he annoyed the children. Finally he lost his job and I was fired, too.

"I want nothing to do with him and I won't do anything to help him." He looked around. "What was the name of the girl he killed?" He was told and he shuddered. "My God," young Fish said, "that's the name he used to scream out when he awoke out of sleep up on Amsterdam Avenue. I never paid much attention to it, because I don't read the papers."

THE ELDER Fish's sleep during the night had been fitful. Then, as this day wore on, between questioning and being taken from one part of headquarters to another, he sat almost silently in his cell, tapping his head with his fingertips. Once in a while he mumbled something, but that was all. At four-thirty in the afternoon, he ate a sandwich, after which he was taken to the regular line-up of criminals—standard procedure. Police, meanwhile, told newsmen that Fish had signed three separate confessions—which he later was to deny, saying he had signed none of them.

Two more or less celebrities were in the line-up room as Fish shuffled up onto the little stage with the height line behind him, but the glare of lights kept him from seeing them —Mrs. Alfred E. Smith and Dr. Allan Roy Dafoe, the pipe-smoking little Canadian doctor who had delivered the Dionne quintuplets. Going to the police line-up to see the little daily drama was a Thing to Do at the time, the same as visiting Night Court as a change from the Stork Club.

Acting Captain Thomas A. Dugan put the questions to Fish.

"Why did you commit this crime?" he said matter-of-factly. In the lights, Fish blinked.

"It occurred to me," he said in his soft voice.

"Did you ever have anything to do with other children?"

Fish shook his head waveringly. "I never had anything to do with another child." The rest of the questions were brief and perfunctory. Fish admitted he had been confined at various times in the mental wards of King's County Hospital in Brooklyn and Bellevue Hospital in Manhattan. Dr. Dafoe leaned forward all during the brief session, so as not to miss any of the questions, but later all he had to say to the reporters was that Fish was "a study" but out of his domain.

After the line-up they took the old man to Captain Stein's office so he could make a detailed statement for District Attorney Frank H. Coyne of Westchester, who was accompanied by Captain Philip J. McQuillan of the Greenburgh police. Fish reported in essence what he had said before, adding a few details and embellishing the telling with graphic gestures, after which he was delivered over to Homicide Court for a routine arraignment on suspicion of homicide. Magistrate Adolph Stern put the hearing over for Friday, December 21, with no bail set, and the New York District Attorney's office said it likely would surrender Fish to Westchester authorities if they returned a murder indictment against him.

WHILE THE old man was being shuttled back and forth from cell to courtroom, a report, or a report of a report, surfaced.

Late in 1930—mid-December—Fish had been picked up by federal authorities on the obscene-letter charge, and in a natural sequence of events had ended up in the psychiatric ward at Bellevue Hospital, where he had been examined by staff members at some length and given the usual psychiatric tests. Now, with Fish in custody, Dr. Menas S. Gregory's report came to light. Dr. Gregory had been director of Bellevue's psychiatric division when Fish was there.

When the examination was completed at that time, Dr. Gregory wrote to the late Judge Frank J. Coleman of United States District Court with this description of Fish:

"Abnormal—a psychopathic personality, with evidence of early senile change, but not insane or a mental defective." His condition, the authority added, was not uncommon in men of his age.

The Bellevue report was prepared after Dr. Attilio La Guardia, Gregory's assistant, had questioned Fish. At that time, the report said, Fish said he had started writing the obscene letters after reading "a bunch of letters a chauffeur found in a garage at Dr. Robert Lamb's sanitarium in Harlem," where Fish was employed as a painter. No, he couldn't explain why he wrote such letters to strangers. No, ten years before, he wouldn't have done it. He had changed, the old man said, because he had met "this pretty tough bunch of fellows up there in Harlem." At night, Fish added, they all stayed pretty much in one room, playing cards, reading or writing letters, "and I just got into the habit."

He was, the suspect added, a steady Episcopalian churchgoer. "How do you reconcile these things with church?" Dr. LaGuardia asked him. "There is no comparison," Fish replied. Summing up, Dr. LaGuardia wrote that Fish was "quiet and cooperative, orderly and normal, no evidence of delusional notions or hallucinatory experiences," with an excellent memory and "signs of sexual psychopathy (sex perversion) which happens to men of his age, but not significant here, because Fish has manifested sex perversion from early life." An accompanying physical examination report said that Fish had arteriosclerosis and a mild nephrotic disorder but that there was nothing seriously wrong with him.

46

This was two years after Grace Budd had been kidnaped, chopped in pieces, and eaten.

OVER THE weekend, the search went on in Westchester. In all, thirty-one bones ranging from one to eight inches were unearthed and Dr. Squire, the medical examiner, ordered that the hunt go on. If—after submission to professors of comparative anatomy at Columbia University—it were proved that the bones were human, he said, several New York City and Connecticut murder cases would be reopened. "We will take no chances," Dr. Squire stated. "In view of Fish's confession, there is no telling what else he has done of a criminal nature—to which he has not confessed."

On Saturday it was announced that two wells on the property would be pumped dry, and the busy activity went on, as hundreds of motorists drove by, with a squad of White Plains traffic policemen shooing away souvenir hunters. One of the visitors to Fish in the Tombs, to which he had been taken now, was Henry J. Case, chairman of the Darien, Connecticut, police board, who wanted to talk with the old man about the skeleton of a four- to six-year-old child, head severed, that had been found in the woods near Darien the previous June. Case reported that Fish simply had kept shaking his head during their talk and was sullen.

Another to come forward was a Rudolph Gabelman, who lived in Elmsford about a mile from the crime. From his story, Fish apparently had at least once returned to the scene of the crime. Gabelman said Fish had lived with him and his family for about a month in 1932, but never had paid his rent. One day two men "who looked like detectives" came to see Fish, and that night the old man and his belongings disappeared from Elmsford. "He still owes us a month's rent," Gabelman added.

In the Tombs, Detective King put questions to Fish about

three other child murders—or at least one disappearance and two murders. In one of the city's most celebrated cases, four-year-old Billy Gaffney of Brooklyn had vanished on February 11, 1927. Then there was the case of the decapitated body found in Darien, and also the murder of fifteen-year-old Mary Ellen O'Connor of Massapequa, Long Island. Inspector Harold King of the Nassau detective force was with Detective King when the latter case was discussed, but no announcement was made of the results, and presumably Fish had denied any complicity in the three cases.

Some policemen continued to search the area of the old house in Greenburgh, digging up five more bones, but their main problem seemed to be in taking care of stalled and skidding cars. A typical December evening in the Northeast, complete with an all-night chilling rain, had left the roadway leading up to the house covered with ice, and the autos of the curious went this way and that on the slippery surface.

That was on Sunday, December 16. On Monday, Detective King came out and told reporters that the old man had admitted having been in Darien in March of the same year and also that he was in Farmingdale, Long Island, at the time Mary Ellen O'Connor was murdered. Meanwhile, the New York County Grand Jury moved to indict Fish on a kidnaping charge, and Walter Ferris, an assistant district attorney in Westchester, said evidence toward a murder indictment would be given to a county grand jury on Thursday. There was some question as to whether the kidnaping charge in New York would hold up, since there was a five-year statute of limitations on such charges, but finally it was decided that since Fish had left the state at various times after 1928 and had lived under an assumed name, the statute did not apply.

By Thursday the Westchester grand jury was in session

and, after hearing thirteen witnesses, it took just two hours to indict Fish for "murder one." The witnesses included Mr. and Mrs. Budd, and the latter broke down and wept when she was asked to identify the little beads Grace had worn, that had been found near the bones of her daughter.

One person who had had something to do with Fish in the past, and another who was quite sure that he had, came forward. In Waterloo, Iowa, a housemaid named Mrs. Estelle Wilcox told police she had married Fish in Waterloo on February 6, 1930, and had lived with him for one week. They had been divorced April 2, 1930, she added, "and I don't care what happens to him." They had met, she said, through a matrimonial agency.

In Brooklyn, a painter named Benjamin Eiseman, twenty-eight, volunteered the information that twelve years before, when he had been sixteen and just two years removed from his native Russia, he had met a man he now believed was Fish, at Battery Park in lower Manhattan. The man had hired him as a painter's helper, Eiseman said, and the two of them had ridden the Staten Island ferry across the Upper Bay, then had taken a train from the town of St. George to a deserted area a half-hour away. There, he said, Fish had left him at a shack and said, "Wait here until I get my tools."

While waiting, Eiseman added, he saw an old Negro who appeared, regarded him, shook his head, and said, "Listen, son, you'd better get out of here. A lot of kids have gone in there and didn't never come out." Eiseman took the hint and got away in a hurry, making his way back to Manhattan. When he told police about the episode of a dozen years before, he was visibly upset.

"I would never forget that face," he said.

On Friday, December 21, under indictment for the murder of Grace Budd, Albert Howard Fish was removed to Eastview Prison in White Plains.

I am become, as it were, a monster
unto many.

—Psalm xxi, 6

5. OF ALL THE crimes known to and la-
beled by man, cannibalism is considered the most degener-
ate, the most shocking. Murder, rape, sodomy, incest—these
are crimes to shock the impressionable and even raise an
eyebrow of the cynical. But man eating man stuns civilized
humanity into silence.

It is hard to believe this horrified aversion to cannibalism
is not inborn.

Yet listen to the *Encyclopedia Americana*:

"The aversion to eating human flesh is not instinctive;
rather, the horror shown by civilized men and by most of
the primitive peoples is a specialized development."

As a matter of fact, the volume goes on, cannibalism is "a
customary, socially-approved practice among certain barba-
rous peoples, of eating flesh. By extension the term is also
applied to animals which eat their own kind." It is possible,
the report goes on, that the earliest humans fed on human
flesh "as on any other," and it seems probable that at least

one of man's early ancestors, the Peking man, brought skulls into caves in China "where the posterior sections were bashed in, presumably to pick out the brains." Certainly there are definite evidences of the practice in long-ago times that may not be quite so ancient as Peking man's.

In the fifth century B.C., for instance, Herodotus wrote that Irish Celts, Scythians, and others were cannibalistic, and Saint Jerome, the monk-scholar who lived three or four hundred years after the Crucifixion, said that on his arrival in the British Isles he found northern Britons who ate human flesh. "Though they had plenty of sheep and cattle," Jerome wrote, "they preferred a ham of the herdsman or a slice of the female breast as a luxury." And, of course, the original Greek term, *anthropophagy*, suggests that the practice goes back into antiquity.

Although in recent centuries cannibalism has been concentrated chiefly in tropical and subtropical areas, it has been found nearly everywhere on earth. In the thirteenth century, Marco Polo reported he had found it in Tibet and Sumatra. According to Abd-Allatif, a Bagdad physician who wrote a contemporary history in that same era, it was rife in all classes of Egyptian society. In North America many primitive Indians were said to have been cannibalistic; indeed, the name Mohawk means "man-eater." At the time of Columbus's disputed discovery of the western world, there were West Indies tribes called Caribales or Canibales, and it was from them that the modern-day name came. In Ecuador and Peru along the eastern Andes, the Jivaro Indians ate human flesh at their victory feasts, and in the early days of exploration of South America, Spaniards found that such meat was considered a delicacy in Amazon country or along the Orinoco. Cannibalism extended from the northern part of that continent all the way up to the Gulf Coast of the land now called the United States.

In the main, however, devouring the ham of the herdsman has been confined in recent centuries to two specific areas, the South Pacific and Africa.

In Polynesia it was for years condoned, even held in high esteem, and there is on record the story of a Fiji chief credited with having eaten nine hundred people. In his book *Cannibal Land,* published in 1922, the explorer Martin Johnson stated he had come upon the tail end of a cannibalistic feast. The natives ran off at the appearance of his party, but in the embers of a fire he found "a charred human head, with rolled leaves plugging the eye-sockets."

Africa, of course, has been most publicized for cannibalism. The fierce Mangbettu tribe once practiced it widely although it does not any longer, and as recently as 1930 it was said to be prevalent among the Vasele in the Congo. The Ubangi were human flesh-eaters, and before they abandoned the practice it was common for a whole group of townspeople to buy a body "wholesale," so to speak, and sell it retail. The Bambala in the Congo added a fillip to cannibalism. They preferred flesh that had been buried for some days; that is, they practiced *necrophagy,* or the robbing of graves and eating the corpses. Cannibalism really started to die away in Africa with the coming of the slave trade. The fiercer tribes found they could get better prices for live slaves from the white man than for dead meat from neighbors.

Now almost all of these cultures put the stress on the ritualistic side of the practice. Killing people and eating their flesh was part of ceremonies such as coming of age or to manhood, or celebrating a battlefield triumph. In his recent *Tradition and Change in African Tribal Life,* Colin M. Turnbull wrote, "In the whole of Africa, there were probably only one or two tribes who actually ate human flesh because they enjoyed it, and we are not even sure about that." And back in 1864, the anthropologist W. Windwood Reade declared that a cannibal was not necessarily ferocious. "He eats his fellow-creatures not because he hates them, but because he likes them," he explained.

Cannibalism has had its defenders, among them Diogenes and Montaigne—and its lucid explainers. In the encyclopedia we are told: "It is quite possible that the abhorrence arose from a combination of fear of the dead, self-projection as a potential victim, and, in later ethical development, considerations of the sanctity of human life."

When you have digested all these references, incidents, and events, however, remember that they are about cultures and people that, in their own *milieu*, were considered normal—whatever that may be.

FREDRIC WERTHAM, M.D., was born Frederick Iganace Wertheimer in 1895, was a graduate of the University of Wurtsberger, studied medicine there and at the University of Erlangen as well as Kings College in London, and took postgraduate studies in Munich. He was for more than twenty years the senior psychiatrist of New York City's Department of Hospitals and in later years founded the Quaker Readjustment Center in New York, devoted solely to sex offenders, and the famous La Fargue Clinic in Harlem, where clients paid twenty-five cents per visit. His career was burgeoning in the early and mid-thirties, and by the forties he was recognized as one of the world's foremost psychiatrists, as well as the author of the books *The Show of Violence* and *A Sign for Cain: An Exploration of Human Violence.* His *Dark Legend: A Study in Murder* was turned into a successful play, and in the fall of 1934, only months before the story of Albert Fish cropped up, his *The Brain as an Organ* was published.

Looking around for the best psychiatrist he could find,

defense counsel James Dempsey came up with Wertham's name. Only a few years before, the genteel but intense Wertham, a bespectacled, mild-mannered man with unshakable convictions, had examined several thousand mental patients at Johns Hopkins Hospital in Baltimore. He was an ideal choice. Dempsey asked him to go to Eastview and examine the old man.

On a cold winter day, Dr. Wertham made his first visit to the Westchester jail, set in an almost bucolic background of trees, lawns, and semiforests, and he had the same first reaction to Fish that others seemed to have. "He looked like a meek and innocuous little old man, gentle and benevolent, friendly and polite," Wertham said. "If you wanted someone to entrust your children to, he would be the one you would choose."

To the old man, Wertham's visit at first was just another one—of just another "head shrinker." Many psychiatrists, for both prosecution and defense, were to examine him before he went to trial. Indeed, after Wertham's first visit he wrote to one of his daughters, "Some doctor came and asked me a million questions," and that was all.

"But when he realized that I was really scientifically interested, was probing into details and going to check them," Wertham said, "was determined to understand him really, his detachment changed to interest. The whole procedure of examination took a long time and a number of sessions. He showed a certain desire to make himself understood and even to try to understand himself. The last time I saw him he said quietly, 'I'll never forget you, doctor.'"

Patiently, carefully, Wertham probed into the dark recesses of Fish's mind.

The old man talked about his family and the considerable mental abnormality in it, and he spoke feelingly about his days in the Washington orphanage from which, he said, he "ran away every Saturday." He told of being a tense, nervous child, and he was candid about being a bed-wetter until he was eleven.

It was when Wertham gently led him into discussion of his sexual life that, the psychiatrist later said, he found it to be "of unparalleled perversity."

The thousands of mental cases that Wertham had examined in Baltimore and New York paled as he dug into Fish's background. "I did research in the psychiatric and criminological literature and found no published case that would even nearly compare with his," Wertham said. "Freud has described the assumed primitive pleasure life of the infant as 'polymorph perverse.' In one of his latest (posthumous) papers he pointed out that when the different phases of the organization of the libido follow each other there are no sharp divisions, but instead a considerable overlapping.

"Fish was a polymorph perverse adult. There was no known perversion that he did not practice and practice frequently."

Wertham found Fish to be, in his own way, a complex character—a man of some intelligence, shrewd and cunning, who told varying stories as they occurred to him, sometimes contradicting, sometimes being astonishingly candid. The psychiatrist picked his way carefully like a skillful broken-field runner through the maze of answers, comments, and philosophies. Wertham decided that there was a definite line of demarcation between Fish's actual deeds as he told of them and his flights of fancy, his daydreams. Gradually he came to know, he felt, when the old man was telling the facts as they were or merely indulging in fantasy.

What seemed ironic—indeed hard to believe—was Fish's obvious concern about his children, all of them grown now, and his grandparental pride in little Gloria DeMarco, of whom he said, "She's twelve years old [she was eleven] and in 7-A. She's a great little dancer; I just idolize her. She's going to take up stage dancing.

"I love children and was always soft-hearted. Murder was not in my heart at all."

Fact—and fancy. Later, Fish was to tell the psychiatrist of his intent to kill, not only Grace Budd but others. And with further irony, Fish said he was upset and angry over being charged with kidnaping. The Budds, he declared, had given him their permission to take Grace with him—so how could there have been any kidnaping?

He analyzed himself off-handedly. After saying he had no particular desire to live, nor any to be killed—"It is a matter of indifference to me—" he added, "I do not think I am altogether right." Wertham asked him bluntly, "Do you mean to say that you are insane?"

"Not exactly," the old man said thoughtfully. "I compare myself a great deal to Harry Thaw in his ways and actions and desires. I never could understand myself."

The reference, of course, was to the deranged slayer of architect Stanford White.

It was to Wertham, finally, that Fish admitted his cannibalism.

HE HAD BEEN surprised, he told the doctor, at the struggle that little Grace put up. "She was a frail-looking child," he explained. "She gave me the surprise of my life. She was losing consciousness and I placed my knee on her chest to squeeze the breath out of her, to get her out of her misery."

When he finally had killed her, he said, he dismembered her. "In a posthumous paper discussing the severed head of the Medusa," Wertham said, "Freud equates symbolically cutting off the head and castration. Fish, who had never read Freud, said in one of his confessions to the police: 'I thought it [Grace] was a boy.'"

As used as he was to the aberrations of the mentally ill, Wertham found himself almost shuddering as he heard Fish describe the eating of Grace's body. "He took parts of her body home with him, cooked them in various ways with carrots and onions and strips of bacon, and ate of them over a period of nine days. During all this time he was in a state of sexual excitement. He ate the flesh during the day and thought about it during the nights," the psychiatrist said.

Wertham found Fish's mien, as he spoke, to be bizarre. "He spoke in a matter-of-fact way, like a housewife describing her favorite methods of cooking," he said. "You had to remind yourself that this was a little girl that he was talking about. But at times his tone of voice and facial expression indicated a kind of satisfaction and ecstatic thrill.

"I said to myself, however you define the medical and legal borders of sanity, this certainly is beyond that border."

It was to Wertham, too, that Fish first spoke of his "messages" and his "visions." Sometimes, he said, he was certain that the voices came from "visions and angels"; at other times, he didn't know where they came from. He heard, he said, words like "stripes," "rewardeth," and "delighteth." " 'Stripes,' " he told Wertham, "means to lash them, you know. I could hear words spoken, and of course a great deal I have read. I could put the words together and see what they meant. Then I made up the rest from what I'd read."

Orson Welles, the actor, has admitted genially that at times when quoting Shakespeare in television or radio appearances, he occasionally has gotten it a bit mixed up, such as slipping a little *King Lear* into *Hamlet*. It was the same sort of thing with Fish, with his own peculiar Biblical passages: "O ye daughter of Babylon." "Blessed is he that rewardeth them as Thou servest us." "Happy is he that taketh Thy little ones and dasheth their heads against the stones." "Blessed is the man who correcteth his son in whom he de-

lighteth with stripes, for great shall be his reward." They
had a ring and almost an authentic air to them, but they
were strange words and thoughts, as if seen through a glass
darkly.

"He felt driven to torment and kill children," Wertham
said. "Sometimes he would gag them, tie them up, and beat
them, although he preferred not to gag them, circumstances
permitting, for he liked to hear their cries. He felt that he
was ordered by God to castrate little boys. 'I had sort of an
idea through Abraham offering his son Isaac as a sacrifice. It
always seemed to me that I had to offer a child for sacrifice,
to purge myself of iniquities, sins, and abominations in the
sight of God. Such a Sodom and Gomorrah!' "

Fish told Wertham that originally he had planned to murder Edward Budd, as well as castrate him. "They asked
me," he said, "if I didn't think it would be a fatal affair. I
said 'That *would* be a fatal affair.' I would have left him in
the house—tied up—and gone back to my room, packed up
my things, and left town." Wertham, listening intently, decided that this was no mere fantasy but an actual plan,
since, he felt, it was just what Fish had done in other cases
where he had castrated or partly castrated small boys before
the Budd episode.

The Budd boy, however, was too big for him and, further,
didn't attract the old man. After he met little Grace, his
thoughts were only of her. He told Wertham that he knew
"that this child would eventually be outraged and tortured
and so forth, and that I should sacrifice her in order to prevent her future outrage. The only interpretation of it that I
could have was that she could be saved in that way."

Despite his candid descriptions of his "messages," Fish
didn't try to say they had anything to do with Grace's murder. "He always mixed up his explanations when he talked
about these messages," Wertham said, "saying both that he

had the desire to do something and that he was commanded to do something. These discrepancies in explanation never bothered him at all."

In his rambling way the old man talked about the times he was "picked up" by the police, adding that on these occasions it usually was because of a complaint by a child. He was incredibly lucky, however, he said, in that: "It never came out. Children don't seem to tell. I always managed to cover it up." He related incident after incident to Wertham, although his normally good memory failed him here and there and he couldn't pinpoint the names of cities or dates. Once he told the psychiatrist about a twelve-year-old girl whom he had met while he was doing a job of painting in a house. "She was very loose in her ways, although only a child," Fish said. "I had her in my room, but what stopped me was the man who had a master key, showing the empty flats. I put her in a closet and put a fifty-pound paint pail in front of the closet. Otherwise I would have been in a fix right there. The manager said he had heard things. He felt like kicking me out. He must have heard the things from some of these children."

Wertham asked him about his habit of sticking needles into himself, and Fish came up with his aforementioned explanations, although he didn't seem to consider them contradictory in any way. His explanations: (1) he did it to punish himself for his acts of evil against others, (2) he got a "sexual kick" out of it, (3) "voices" told him to purge himself of sin through self-torture, (4) he did it to ease the pain from a hernia (he was operated on for this, after the Budd killing), and (5) he felt that perforating his intestines might kill him, which occasionally he felt he deserved.

Now and then he would interrupt his tales and say lucidly to Wertham, "I'm just queer. I don't understand it myself. It is up to you to find out what is wrong with me."

59

Endlessly, it seemed, he went on about his attacks on children, and Wertham figured that there had been more than a hundred of them. "I always had a desire to inflict pain on others and to have others inflict pain on me," he said. "I always seemed to enjoy everything that hurt. The desire to inflict pain, that is all that is uppermost."

When his visits came to an end, Wertham drew up a list of Fish's perversions. These were later to be introduced into the court testimony, but they were disallowed by the presiding justice. They were:

1. *Sadism:* the infliction of pain and bodily injury for sexual gratification.

2. *Masochism:* having others inflict pain on oneself in order to obtain sexual pleasure.

3-4. *Active and passive flagellation:* whipping and being whipped.

5-6. *Self-castration and castration:* the cutting off of one's own genitals or those of another.

7. *Exhibitionism:* showing oneself in the nude, usually done when standing in the window.

8. *Voyeur acts:* peeping and looking at others who are either nude or who perform sexual acts.

9. *Picqueur acts:* sticking needles into others or into oneself for sexual motives.

10. *Paedophilia:* sexual acts with children.

11. *Homosexuality:* sexual relations with one's own sex.

12. *Penilinctio:* application of mouth to penis.

13. *Fellatio:* same as *penilinctio.*

14. *Cunnilingus:* application of mouth to female genitals.

15. *Anilingus:* application of mouth to rectum.

16. *Coprophagia:* eating of feces.

17. *Undinism:* playing with urine; for example, urination into another person's mouth.

18. *Fetishism:* abnormal preference for one part of the body, such as buttocks, or for inanimate objects.

19. *Cannibalism:* the eating of human flesh.

20. *Hyperotism (or hyperhedonism):* abnormal intensity of the sexual instinct.

The prince of darkness is a gentleman.

—*King Lear*, III, 4

6. THE DISAPPEARANCE of Grace Budd on Sunday, May 27, 1928, was a much-publicized news story at the time, but not an extraordinary one. Children always were disappearing, as they always have. The world and the nation had other fish to fry. She was just another missing person.

From the Arctic, General Umberto Nobile's dirigible *Italia* bound on a polar expedition reported itself in distress and sent out SOS signals. The papers said United States tourists spent nearly two billion dollars abroad in 1927. In Chicago, the Sanitary Cleaning and Dyeing Company took Al Capone in as a partner, and suddenly the gang violence against cleaners and dyers stopped. On Broadway, Helen Hayes was playing *Coquette* at the Maxine Elliott, and Mae West was appearing in *Diamond Lil* at the Royale. Showers fell across most of New York and, if you wanted to catch a movie, you could drop in at the Rialto and catch *The Street of Sin* with Emil Jannings and Fay Wray—her glory days as King Kong's inamorata still ahead of her.

Methodically, routinely, the police started to work on the Budd case—but, even with promising leads here and there, they kept running into dead ends.

A dozen detectives from the West 20th Street precinct house searched all the homes and cellars in the Chelsea neighborhood where the Budds lived. There was a report that "Frank Howard," the visiting gentleman, had used an automobile with a Pennsylvania license. The word got out that Frank Howard was bowlegged, and this fact was duly noted on the missing-persons flyers. On Tuesday, June 5, a Brooklyn woman reported that a man resembling the publicized description of Howard had started off with her three-year-old son at 6:00 P.M. on the past Sunday—a time when Fish already had used his tools of death—and, when she had cried out, apologized to her and then took off in a car with a young woman and young man in it.

The next day, police questioned two more persons and let them go. One was a genuine, full-blown "mystery woman," so integral a part of murder cases. She was a Mrs. Heming of Union City, New Jersey, who had gone to the Budd home the Tuesday after Grace's disappearance. Mrs. Heming said she had known a Mamie McKenna as a girl who had married an Edward Budd, and she had gone to see if it was the same woman she had known. Then there was a Miriam Whitney of Brooklyn, who had been "acting rather mysteriously" around the Budd home but she, too, was released after questioning. The "kook" messages started coming in. Mrs. Budd received two postcards, both in the same writing, one of which said starkly, "All little Girl is to cellar and into water," but police ultimately disregarded them.

Fish seemed to have covered his tracks exceedingly well, and the detectives were going around in circles. On Sunday, June 10, for instance, two weeks after Grace had vanished, they announced they had pretty much given up on the theory that the little girl had been lured away by a demented man. What they felt now, they said, was that Howard was a member of a kidnaping gang—although why the gang should kidnap a girl from a very poor family was not gone into. Around the Budd neighborhood other children said they had seen Grace taken to an automobile with a young man at the wheel. Still checking the area minutely, police came up with the delicatessen that had sold Frank Howard the cottage cheese he had told the Budds came from his farm in Farmingdale. That didn't help the search a great deal.

On Monday, June 11, Mrs. Budd reported to the detectives that her son had seen a blue sedan patrolling their street on that infamous Sunday, driven by a young man in a brown suit, with no hat, who kept his face averted. The car, she added, had a 6-V license plate. But trickles of information such as this, most of it in error, gave police no new leads, and gradually the story faded from the newsprint and even lapsed into a more or less routine case for the Missing Persons Bureau. The Republicans went into their national convention in Kansas City and nominated Herbert Hoover for the presidency on the first ballot. The trimotor monoplane *Friendship* flew from Newfoundland to Wales in a little under twenty-two hours, landing out of gas with two men and a woman named Amelia Earhart, who thus became the first woman to fly the Atlantic Ocean.

The months went by and then the years. In the end a cockroach led police to Albert Howard Fish.

THE MISSING PERSONS BUREAU never really gives up on any one of its searches. Sometimes the old cases get shuffled to the rear, but the head men somehow always are aware of them and, better than most, they remember names, voices, faces. So the Grace Budd case, over a period of six years, never really was closed. Now and then a new spoor would be uncovered and detectives would follow it dutifully until it petered out.

As a matter of fact, twice the law suspected it might have its man, aided by Mrs. Budd's penchant for, as her husband noted wryly, identifying nearly everybody and anybody as Frank Howard.

A janitor named Charles Edward Pope was so identified by her not too long after the incident and spent a hundred and nine days in jail but, when he came up for trial, Mrs. Budd said she couldn't say for sure that he was the man, and the judge ordered an acquittal. In 1931, three years after the abduction-slaying, a man named Alfred Corchell was arrested in Florida and extradited to New York, where a grand jury indicted him—again on the strength of Mrs. Budd's identification. Once again the charge was dismissed, for the same reason.

There were, naturally, letters, cards, and messages. After a while, since they all seemed to fall into the "crank" category, the Budds didn't even bother to read them but simply sent them along to the MPB.

Detective King, in charge of the Budd file, had one fairly valuable item in his dossier. Shortly after Grace had been taken, his men had come up with the handwritten copy of the telegram Fish had sent to the Budds, in which he said he had been detained in New Jersey on business and wouldn't return to the Budd home until the following Sunday.

Armed with that handwriting specimen, King patiently went over the various letters that trickled in. In the second week of November, 1934, the Budds sent him one that had been mailed at 1:30 A.M., November 11, from the Grand Central Annex Post Office in Manhattan—and King had hit pay dirt. The writing was the same.

It was a strange, at times almost incoherent letter—but it had an authentic ring to it:

"My dear Mrs. Budd—

In 1894 a friend of mine shipped as a deck hand on the steamer Tacoma, Captain John Davis. They sailed from San Francisco for Hong Kong, China. On arriving there, he and two others went ashore and got drunk. When they returned, the boat was gone. At that time there was a famine in China. *Meat of any form* was from $1 to 3 dollars a pound. So great was the suffering among the very poor, that all children under 12 were sent to the butchers to be cut up and sold for food in order to keep others from starving. A boy or girl under 14 was not safe in the streets. You could go in any shop and ask for steak—chops—or stew meat. Part of the naked body of a boy or girl would be brought out and just what you wanted cut from it. A boy or girls behind which is the sweetest part of the body and sold as veal cutlet brought the highest price. John staid there so long he acquired a taste for human flesh. On his return to New York, he stole two boys, one 7 one 11. Took them to his home stripped them naked, tied them in a closet. Then burned everything they had on. Several times every day and night he spanked them—to make their meat fresh and tender. First he killed the 11 yr. old boy, because he had the fattest ass and of course the most meat on it. Every part of his body was cooked and eaten except head—bones and guts. He was Roasted in the oven (all of his ass) boiled, broiled, fried, stewed. The little boy was next, went the same way. At that time I was living at 409 e. 100 st., near—night side. He told me so often how good human flesh was I made up my mind to taste it. On Sunday, June 3—1928 I called on you at 406 W. 15 St. brought you put cheese—strawberries. We had lunch. Grace sat in my lap and kissed me. I made up my mind to eat her. On the pretense of taking her to a party. You said yes she could go. I took her to an empty house in Westchester I had already picked out. When we got there,

66

I told her to remain outside. She picked wild flowers. I went upstairs and stripped all my clothes off. I knew if I did not I would get her blood on them. When all was ready I went to the window and called her. Then I hid in a closet until she was in the room. When she saw me all naked she began to cry and tried to run down stairs. I grabbed her and she said she would tell her mama. First I stripped her naked. How she did kick—bite and scratch. I choked her to death then cut her in small pieces so I could take my meat to my rooms, cook and eat it. How sweet and tender her little ass was roasted in the oven. It took me 9 days to eat her entire body. I did not fuck her tho I could of had I wished. She died a virgin."

CAPTAIN AYRES, the Missing Persons Bureau chief, worked over the letter with King when it had been returned from the police laboratory after being tested in many ways. The only sizable clue—since there was no address or signature—was a monogram design on the rear flap of the envelope. It had been crossed out with a pencil—heavily but not heavily enough that the initials ultimately couldn't be made out.

It was almost as if the man who wrote the letter had decided to leave a trail—even though a very small trail—to himself.

The initials in the design were P.C.B.A. "Check with the phone company," Captain Ayres told King. "They should be able to tell you what P.C.B.A. stands for." And so they were. The initials were those of the Private Chauffeurs' Benevolent Association, with offices at 627 Lexington Avenue in midtown Manhattan. Sergeants Sheridan and Hamill were sent to the group's offices, taking with them a photostatic copy of the letter to Mrs. Budd. An Arthur Ennis was the president of the P.C.B.A.

Sergeant Sheridan asked Ennis if he knew a man named Frank Howard and whether he was or had been a member of the organization. "No. No Frank Howard is in our archives," Ennis said. The investigators then asked to see the forms that members of the association had to fill out, on joining—but after plowing through all of them, they found no handwriting to match that on the letter.

"Is your stationery used only by the association," Sergeant Hamill asked, "or do members have access to it?"

"Only by the office," Ennis said, "although I suppose a member might use an envelope once in a while."

The description of Howard, as it had been so widely circulated six years before, was shown the group president, but Ennis couldn't remember such a man. It seemed like one more dead end. When Captain Ayres got their report late in the afternoon, he told them to return to the Lexington Avenue offices the next day and talk with every member of the P.C.B.A. "Someone must have given Howard that envelope," he said. Sergeant Hamill scratched his head.

"Suppose one of the association's members is a nut?" he asked. "Suppose he sent the letter and didn't have anything to do with the girl's disappearance?"

"Six years after the murder?" Captain Ayres said softly. "No. There hasn't been a letter like this for five years."

The policemen went back to Lexington Avenue the next day. On the club bulletin board, they tacked the Howard description. They started interviewing as many P.C.B.A. members as could be rounded up. The officers were sitting in a nearby cafeteria having luncheon when they were approached by a middle-aged man in overalls. "About that envelope," he started tentatively, and the men motioned to him to sit down and talk.

The man said his name was Bryan (although later at Fish's trial King identified him as a "Lee Sicoski") and he was a janitor-porter employed by the association. "About that envelope," he said, "I know you're looking for the guy who disappeared with that little girl. I want to do anything I can to help. But I don't want to get into any trouble. I don't want to lose my job."

King told him that, if he was of help, they'd help him and see to it he didn't lose his job. Bryan nodded. "All right," he said. "I swiped some of those envelopes along with some writing paper. It saved me a few cents and the association would never miss it."

He lived now with his sister in Brooklyn, Bryan went on —but he had left some of the envelopes behind in his old rooming house at 200 East 52nd Street.

Room Eleven.

In one of his various confessions, Fish said later that, when he lived in the rooming house, he one day had seen a cockroach climbing a wall. He had tracked it up the wall and onto a cupboard shelf, where he killed it. And found the chauffeurs' union envelopes.

FRIEDA SCHNEIDER was the landlady at the 52nd Street rooming house, and when Sergeant Sheridan asked her if she knew Frank Howard (as the policeman knew him) she said no. And no one was in Room Eleven, she replied. "About a month ago," King said to her, "the tenant of Room Eleven, whose name was Bryan, moved out. We want to know who has occupied that room since."

There had been only one roomer there, the woman said. His name was Albert H. Fish. She described him—in his sixties, mustachioed, gray hair, black suit, black hat.

Frank Howard.

Albert H. Fish.

"Sometimes," she added, "he stayed in his room for long periods at a time. On other occasions he stayed out all night. He told me he was a house painter."

Asked for a sample of Fish's handwriting, she produced a receipt he had signed for two keys to the room, which he had received for a cash deposit to insure against their loss. When King asked if Fish had left a forwarding address, she said no but "if you want to see him, he'll be here around the first of the month." That was when he regularly received a check from his son, who was a Civilian Conservation Corps worker based in North Carolina.

The New York City Police Department took over Room Eleven—and had a man there every minute of every day. Meanwhile, the receipt signed by Fish was taken to the departmental handwriting expert. The writing matched that on the letter to the Budds.

The letter from the younger Fish arrived from North Carolina on December 5, four days after the first of the month —but no Fish. The vigil went on for another week. At 10 A.M. on the morning of December 13, Fish came. King was the man on duty. He went downstairs to the foyer and looked at the small, gray, innocent-looking man, and arrested him. There was one small incident. Fish casually reached into his upper left vest pocket and came out with a razor blade, but King grabbed his wrist tightly and he dropped it. There were other blades in the pocket.

> . . . he that hides a dark soul and foul
> thoughts, Benighted walks under the
> mid-day sun; Himself his own dun-
> geon.
>
> —Milton

7. ● BEHIND BARS at last, Albert Fish made up to a half-dozen "confessions"—no one knew how many exactly—to various law-enforcement operatives. Of them all, the one to P. Francis Marro, an assistant district attorney, was the most graphic and seemingly the most accurate. It was made December 13, 1934.

Fish began by saying that he lived at 55 East 128th Street in Manhattan and that in 1928, at the time of the Budd episode, he had lived at 409 East 100th Street. He was not living then with his wife, Anna, he went on, and he hadn't worked for eight weeks before his arrest now in 1934. His last job, he noted with some wistfulness, had been at Central Park West and 94th Street.

"Did you kidnap this little girl, Grace Budd, and kill her?" Marro asked.

"Yes."

He told of his second visit to the Budds. He had, he said, bought a "sort of cooking pot" at a peddler's stand, "filled it with pot cheese and I brought a box of strawberries." He wrapped the cleaver, knife, and saw in a red-and-white striped piece of awning and went downtown to the Budds' basement apartment. When he left there with Grace, they went to an elevated railway station, took a train to Sedgewick Avenue in the Bronx, changed to one that went to the Van Cortlandt Park station, and there took a train to Westchester. Two miles north of White Plains, they got off and, after Grace had hurriedly gone back to the train for "the package you left, Mr. Howard," they walked along the railroad track to "what you call Dublin Road," and then they made their way to Wisteria Cottage.

A flat-roofed, decaying, sad-looking cottage, the place was surrounded by sparse trees along the north side that reached past windows almost to the roof. There was a sagging porch and scrub brush everywhere. A narrow hallway led upstairs to the northwest corner room on the second floor, where there were shadeless windows and a huge closet with double doors, divided by a post.

"Right opposite the room in which the crime took place," Fish said, "is another room. I stepped in that room and shut the door until she got to the head of the stairs. Then I stepped out. When she saw me, she tried to run back. She saw me in that state."

"What state?"

"I was undressed. Completely naked. Yes. So when she saw me in that state, she ran down the stairs. I grabbed her. She said she would tell her mother. I took her into this opposite room, where I had canvas spread on the floor and laid her down as the crime took place."

"What did you do when you laid her down?"

"Choked her until she was absolutely dead."

"With your hands?"

"Yes."

"Where did you get her?"

"By the throat. Dragged her in, laid her on the floor, pressed my knee on her chest to make sure that I would kill her that much quicker. Then I took a knife and slit her throat. Meantime, I had picked up a fifty-pound paint pot that holds fifty pounds of lead. I placed that under her head. She had long hair and that soaked up most of the blood. The blood dropped into the pot. After it was there, I threw the pot out. After, I cut her body into three pieces. Cut her head off, through the middle, above the navel. The rest was her legs and the edge of her body."

"Did you undress her before this?"

"Yes."

"When did you do this?"

"After I choked her."

Fish then digressed momentarily and went back to where they had approached Wisteria Cottage. "On the way up to the house," he said, "it was kind of warm, so I said 'Take off your hat and coat.' She did. I rolled the hat under the coat and put it under a rock. The water had formed an aperture running down the hill, to put a package there."

He returned to the killing. He had, he said, taken Grace's severed head out to the privy.

"There was a board stuck out from the end of the privy," Fish went on, "that was clean, and I took her shoes, the pair of white shoes, laid them there so they would not be seen by anybody using the toilet, and I laid her head on top of another board so that it would not get down in the muss. Then I took the middle part of her body and legs and stuck them behind the door, shut the door to hide them. Then I went into the yard, wiped the blood off my hands."

After which, the old man continued, he returned to his

rooms in East 100th Street. He made no mention of taking parts of the body with him. Four days later, "I returned to the same house. The body had just begun to have a noticeable odor." He took the two parts still in the room, threw them out the window, and then, going downstairs and outside, picked them up and took them to a stone wall to the side and rear of the cottage.

"I laid the feet towards one place," he said, "the middle part of her body fitting in with that. Then I went back to the toilet. Her hair was stiff with blood. I took that out and laid it towards the wall, so the body was as near complete as could, after being cut up."

"Did you have to dig anything?"

"No, I didn't do any digging at all."

"Did you cover it?"

"No. In fact, I was taking a chance on being seen. I didn't spend any more time in the neighborhood than I could. Then I went back home." On his way back to the train, he said, "I met a Captain McQuillan of the Westchester police."

"Did you tell him anything about it?"

"No."

"Did you commit any rape on her?"

"It never entered my mind."

Fish said that, when he and Grace had gone by train up to Westchester, he had bought only a ticket and a half—no round-trip tickets. He bought his return trip ticket at the White Plains station.

"When you bought a ticket and a half, what did you have in your mind?"

"To do just what I did."

"To kill her?"

"Yes."

Almost gratuitously, the old man talked about his first arrest "about 1902 or 1903," on Long Island. "I was manager of the Patchogue Cooperative stores in Patchogue, Long Island," he said. "I did all the banking. So then the fellow came in from R. C. Williams, one of the wholesale grocery houses, and asked me if we had any money. We were heavily in debt to them. He said 'I will tell you, the first of the week if we don't get a check, slam bang goes the door.' I figured out, if this is the case—when they told me they engaged me, they said they were doing thirty thousand cash and two-thirds of it credit—I figured I would take the eight hundred and skip. They got me in Long Island City and I got from one to five years in Sing Sing."

Fish mentioned but did not elaborate on his 1930 arrest for writing obscene letters. However, police came up with a statement that one of his married daughters, Mrs. Gertrude DeMarco, had made at that time. She didn't know exactly why he was arrested, she said.

"He acted all right to me," Mrs. DeMarco said at that time. "He has been living by himself in a furnished room since September. My mother died fourteen years ago. [This was not true, of course.—Ed.] There were six children. He took quite an interest in us. Beginning about two, three years ago, he began to live by himself. During the past year he has been unable to find steady employment. Before that, he had always managed to find fairly regular employment as a painter. Lately, we noticed that he didn't want to be bothered but he was always interested in the family. His memory was good. He wasn't unreasonable. He still continued to be considerate."

IN HIS CELL at Eastview, the old man was quiet, cheerful, and morose by turns. Various psychiatrists besides Wertham came to see him, and he submitted to them almost meekly. At first one of his sons hired a Port Jefferson, Long Island, attorney named Carl J. Heyser to represent him but, as the weeks wore on, Fish became convinced that he needed a Westchester lawyer to defend him capably in a Westchester court, so he hired James Dempsey. Fish had no funds, of course, and the state paid Dempsey's fee.

Only one part of jail life really bothered him. In an adjoining cell was a youth named Lawrence Clinton Stone, who was awaiting trial for having stuffed a little girl into a furnace in Mount Vernon, New York, and Stone's habit of cursing loudly at all hours upset Fish. On January 13, he wrote to Warden George A. Casey and complained: "It's the most filthy language I ever heard. I can't read my Bible with a cursing maniac in the cell next to me."

Indeed, a good deal of Fish's time in jail was spent writing letters. Most of them were to his children. On January 8, for example, he wrote to his son John to say, "I have never been able to explain what came over me and I never will.

"The deed never should have been done," he scribbled to his son, "but now it can't be undone. I lay all my troubles to the day eighteen years ago when I returned home and found you children motherless. I have never been the same since. I never before harmed the hair of the head of man, woman or child, or of any living thing. Had I been in my right mind God who alone knows all knows I would not be here."

On January 15, in a second letter to Warden Casey, Fish said that, when he had been detained in Bellevue in 1930, "I done my best to *prove* to Dr. Gregory that I was *sane*. I have never tried to make any one think other wise . . . a man with no teeth in Jail is better off dead. I have lived my life am old weak tired of it."

He wrote to his daughter Gertrude DeMarco on January 17: "All I hope for, all I want to live for, is to be able to go in court, that I may tell what a Bitch of a mother all of you had, the kind of wife I had. Tell her for me, the day I go on the stand she will wish she had never been born. You know *what* a memory I have. I never forget."

Gertrude apparently was one of his favorite children. On January 28 he wrote to her again, saying, "In one of your first letters to me, you spoke of Christmas night 1933. Yes dear Gertie I remember that night. How we all sat near the Radio in the front room and listened to the music. We heard choir boys singing in England Germany and all over." And on February 19, he wrote her again: "No matter *what* the result may be, you see I am better off. No one wants an old man."

During the newspaper publicity on the case, the name of Mary Nicholas, seventeen, one of the seven children of Mrs. Myra Nicholas of Bartlett, Ohio, cropped up. She told police that Fish had visited her widowed mother in 1929, married her (the mother), and had vanished a week later. To Mary, Fish wrote from Eastview:

"So my sweet little big girlie will be 18 on the 28th. I wish I could be there, you know what you would get from *your daddy*. I would wait until you were in bed, then give you 18 good hard smacks on your bare behind." Then, in what seemed a complete *non sequitur* in the letter, he noted, "There is one of the largest pools in the U.S. in the West Side Y.M.C.A., 8th Av. and 57 St. Sometimes there are over 200 men and boys, *all of* them naked. Any boy or man can go in and see them for 25¢."

THE OLD MAN read the papers daily, showing considerable interest in the accounts of his upcoming trial, and incidentally he learned that a young man named Howard Hughes had flown from one coast of America to another in nine hours twenty-seven minutes and ten seconds, setting a world speed record for a plane of 352.338 miles per hour. In England King George V had died at seventy in the twenty-

77

sixth year of his reign, and was succeeded by a slight, rather dashing Edward VIII. In Joliet Prison in the Midwest, Richard Loeb had been slashed to death by a fellow convict, eleven years after he and Nathan Leopold had killed fourteen-year-old Bobby Franks in the so-called "thrill slaying." A Princeton astronomer said the earth was losing its oxygen, and Dr. Nicholas Murray Butler of Columbia University warned Japan its military policy would fail. An actor named Laurence Olivier broke his ankle on the London stage, and in Germany Catholic bishops ordered that prayers be said for the return of the Saar to the fatherland. Clark Gable and Joan Crawford were starring in the film *Forsaking All Others*, and in Flemington, New Jersey, Bruno Richard Hauptmann was on trial for the kidnap-murder of Charles Augustus Lindbergh, Jr.

There was a touch of irony. On Monday, March 4, the name of Representative Hamilton Fish was advanced as a Republican presidential candidate.

James Dempsey made several visits to the jail to confer with his client. Later he talked with newsmen and left no doubt that his defense would be the expected not-guilty-by-reason-of-insanity. "Fish will be his own best witness," the attorney told the reporters, shaking his head sadly. "All the terrible, foul, filthy, and ferocious things he has done will be told the jurors by Fish's own lips."

As the trial date neared, the old man seemed to grow more nervous. How he obtained the material was never made clear, but at one point he again stuffed alcohol-soaked cotton into his rectum and badgered his guards for matches, which they didn't provide. The guards were on an around-the-clock basis. This was one prisoner the state didn't want found hanging in his cell. Fish prayed any number of times each day, and he seemed upset because *The News* of New York referred to him as "the sixty-five-year-old ogre." His actions became queerer and queerer, and Warden Casey reported candidly that he thought Fish was "putting on an act."

On Sunday, March 10, the day before the trial was to begin in the County Courthouse in White Plains, Fish had soup for luncheon. There was a chicken bone in the soup, some three inches or so long—and at four o'clock in the afternoon, the guards heard moaning from the cell. They found the old man with his abdomen slightly slashed by the bone, which he had spent several hours sharpening on the concrete floor of the cell. The cut was only superficial, and a small bandage was applied. "I was just going after the needles," Fish mumbled to his jailers.

DEMPSEY WAS playing it by ear, so to speak. He had a good rough idea of what his defense would be, once court began, but he was busy sorting out possibilities, gathering witnesses, considering strategy. He candidly admitted to associates that one item puzzled him: What exactly should he do with Albert Fish? Let him testify? Keep him off the stand? Use him in which way, to make the jury understand what Dempsey felt deeply—that the old man was, any way you wanted to look at it, insane.

Fish himself wasn't much help. In fact, at one point during his stretch at Eastview, he sat down and in his neat, fairly legible writing, turned out a five-page message to the attorney—in which, either by canny design or for God knows what other reason, he as much as admitted that the Gaffney boy's murder was his work, too.

"There is a public dumping ground in Riker Ave., Astoria," Fish wrote to Dempsey. "All kinds of junk has been thrown there for years.

"Here is my plan: some years ago I lived at 228 E. 81, top floor front. Suppose I confess to *you* that I did ———— the

79

Gaffney boy [Note: the verb was left out by Fish]. In same manner I did the B girl. I am charged with the crime anyhow and many really believe *I did*. I will *admit* the motorman *who positively identified* me as getting off his car with a small boy, was *correct*. I can tell you at that time I was looking for a suitable place to do the job.

"Not satisfied there, I brought him to the Riker Ave. dumps. There is a *house* that stands alone, not far from where I took him. A few yrs. ago I painted this house for the man who owns it. He is in the auto wrecking business. I forget his name but my son Henry can tell you, because he bought a car from him. This man's father lives in the house. Gene, John, Henry helped me paint the house. There were at that time a number of old autos along the road.

"I took the G boy there. Stripped him naked and tied his hands and feet and gagged him with a piece of dirty rag I picked out of dump. Then I burned his clothes. Threw his shoes in the dump. Then I walked back and took trolley to 59 St. at 2 a.m. and walked from there home.

"Next day about 2 p.m., I took tools . . . [unintelligible at this point], a good heavy cat-o-nine tails. Home made. Short handle. Cut one of my belts in half, slit these half in six strips about 8 in. long.

"I whipped his bare behind till the blood ran from his legs. I cut off his ears—nose—slit his mouth from ear to ear. Gouged out his eyes. He was dead then. I stuck the K [knife?] in his belly and held my mouth to his body and drank his blood.

"I picked up four old potato sacks and gathered a pile of stones. Then I cut him up. I had a grip with me. I put his nose, ears and a few slices off his belly in grip. Then I cut him thru the middle of his body. Just below his belly button. Then thru his legs about 2 in. below his behind. I put this in my grip with a lot of paper. I cut off the head—feet—arms—hands and the legs below the knee.

80

"This I put in sacks weighted with stones, tied the ends and threw them into the pools of slimy water you will see all along road going to North Beach. Water is 3 to 4 ft. deep. They sank at once.

"I came home with my meat. I had the front of his body I liked best. His monkey and pee wees and a nice little fat behind to roast in the oven and eat. I made a stew out of his ears—nose—pieces of his face and belly. I put onions, carrots, turnips, celery, salt and pepper. It was good.

"Then I split the cheeks of his behind open, cut off his monkey and pee wees and washed them first. I put all in a roasting pan, lit the gas in the oven. Then I put strips of bacon on each cheek of his behind and put in the oven. Then I picked 4 onions and when meat had roasted about ¼ hr., I poured about a pint of water over it for gravy and put in the onions. At frequent intervals I basted his behind with a wooden spoon. So the meat would be nice and juicy.

"In about 2 hr. it was nice and brown, cooked thru. I never ate any roast turkey that tasted half as good as his sweet fat little behind did. I eat every bit of the meat in about four days. His little monkey was as sweet as a nut, but his pee-wees I could not chew. Threw them in the toilet.

X X X X [Fish's X's]

"You can put my children *wise* as to the above and *if necessary put me* on the stand.

"I can relate the details just as if I were talking about *the weather*.

"The place I have described is just *such a one* to do an act of this kind. How about calling in several reporters and tell them that I told you God told me to purge myself of this sin and depend on his Mercy? Lead them down to the dump. *They will bite hard.* What a sensation. Gene, John, Henry, who worked with me on the house nearby can tell of same. Or do you think I ought to call in Father Mallet of Grace

P.E. Church, White Pl. and *confess to him?* Then you let it loose.

"Write down just what *you* want me to do. If it will be of any good, you can get my record from prison office. It shows *emergency call* about 7 p.m., Cell 1-B-14, Warden Casey and dr. (symptoms of lead poison).

"While in Police Hdqurs., Dec. 13-14, had not as *yet* made confessions to any one. When officer F. W. King left room I was kicked hard in my stones as I sat in chair, by Sgt. Fitzgerald. I can point him out to *you* in court. He said to me, even tho you are an old man, if you don't come clean, I'll take you downstairs and use a length of rubber hose on you. *You* take at least one shot at him in court *for me.*

"Get *torture paddle* I made from officer King. He has it. Shows state of mind. Board with tacks driven thru it."

DEMPSEY WENT over and over the written statement in a state of almost total bewilderment. *Did* Fish kill and eat the Gaffney boy? His description of the macabre scene was almost too good to be faked—and yet, there were Fish's later comments in the note, asking the lawyer to "write down just what you want me to do." And his suggestions about confessing to the White Plains priest, or telling newspaper reporters all about the supposed slaying and cannibalism. And, if you went along with Fish to the extent you felt he *did* perpetrate the act, what about his statement that the Riker Avenue dump "is just such a one to do an act of this kind." Was Fish trying to tell him, look, even if I didn't do it, who's to know? It could have been done. The time and place were right. And Fish's almost gleeful comment on how the reporters, once given this ghoulish story, would "bite hard," and "what a sensation" it would be. Was it all real, was it just another of the fancies that went through Albert Fish's strange mind—or was he simply, shrewdly, trying to help build a case of insanity for himself?

82

Dempsey didn't know, couldn't know. But as he read and reread the five sides of neatly penciled description, one thing seemed more sure to him than ever. Albert Fish was mad. There could be no doubt, no doubt at all.

Men never do evil so completely and
cheerfully as when they do it from religious conviction.

—Blaise Pascal, *Pensées*

8. WHEN ONE speaks of insanity, which
was to be Fish's line of defense, it must be remembered that
there is no such thing.

Not medically. Legally, yes. Medically there are only
manias, psychoses, phobias, and all the gray shades in between—but the word insanity is not in the medical diction-
aries.

Back in medieval Europe, one of the terms for mental disorder was "devil sickness," applied particularly to monks
and nuns who had, in today's *patois*, gone around the bend.
But from then until now, medicine has not come up with
any all-inclusive label.

But we are dealing in this case with the law, so suppose
we use the term insanity, just for clarity? Well, there are,
then, X number of causes of insanity.

Some of the causes are physical, bringing about what the
doctors call *traumatic* psychoses. A blow on the head can

destroy brain tissue and, if a considerable portion is destroyed, *dementia* may result. Cerebral tumors can bring about the same sort of effect.

Old age can bring about impairment of brain function, or *senile dementia*, which follows changes in the brain's nerve cells. The syphilis spirochete can cause *dementia paralytich* or, in the lay term, paresis, the illness that killed Al Capone, the gangster. *Encephalitis* can cause permanent brain damage, attacking the midbrain.

Psychoses can be caused by infections, poisons, and exhaustion, and even a glandular change can be deadly. For instance, a deficiency of *thyroid* gland can change one's personality; indeed, if it is present at birth, the person can be a *cretin*. If it evolves in adult life, the ailment is called *myxedema*, or torpor.

Alcohol can bring about a disorder: It can cause acute *alcoholic hallucinosis*. Then there are the emotional disorders such as manic-depressive psychosis and involutional melancholia. Above all, there is the mystery of psychiatry, *dementia praecox*. This is the term, cloudy even today, that has the common denominator of dissociation, or splitting, of personality. The individual lives in a dream world. The commonest of all psychoses, it even runs all the way down to absentmindedness, its mildest form. And its victims may be merely what are known as constitutional psychopaths—not psychotic, actually, but so unstable emotionally and temperamentally as to be unable to adjust fully to life around them.

Paranoia is among the least prevalent psychoses, but it includes exaggeration of constitutional tendencies, amplification of personality without signs of conflict, a preservation of contact with reality, egocentricity or exaggeration of affectivity, logical development of delusions upon false premises, submission to authority, sound systematization in line with tendencies, and ingenuous methods of defense. Or, in all, a warped mind that still manages to operate with generally good and intense intellectual activity . . . yet in a crooked manner.

Before we leave these confusing technical terms, a word about the "castration complex," which has intrigued psychiatrists from the word go. Dr. Louis L. London, an expert on abnormal sexual behavior, has discussed it at length, quoting Stekel as saying, "It is jealous fantasy of the son to destroy the father, for which he later repents and is conscience-stricken and wishes to castrate himself." And according to London, Freud regarded the will to power as nothing more than a symbol for the longing to castrate, while Adler looked on it as "a form of elemental will." Castration was prevalent in primitive man's day, when he fought for women and emasculated his enemies to prevent them from exercising their sexual power. The ancient Persians, too, used to castrate young men and boys of their vanquished enemies.

Finally, to tie our psychotic lesson into a tidy package, there are the words of Morris Ploscowe, a New York City magistrate and author of *Sex and the Law*, dealing with the legal aspects of sex matters. According to Magistrate Ploscowe, a New York City study of the matter didn't find that most persons committing sex crimes were persistent offenders but "did call attention to the fact that there is a small group of individuals charged with sex crime who are abnormal mentally and who *are* persistent offenders."

"Here," the magistrate wrote, "is the group from which sex killers may be drawn. Such individuals undoubtedly represent a very great danger to the women and children of the community in which they live.

"How great the danger may be is illustrated by the case of Albert Fish."

Insanity, then, exists only in the eyes of the law. And

when Albert Fish went to trial in White Plains, New York, the law recognized only one criterion of it: Did he know right from wrong?

WESTCHESTER COUNTY in the early and mid-thirties still had its reputation as "the richest county in the world." Adjoining New York City on its southern boundary, it was full of grassy, luxurious, manicured communities such as Bronxville, Scarsdale, and the shore towns of Port Chester and Mamaroneck. A few junior executives and a fairly large middle-class group filled out the population, but most of the metropolitan wealthy lived in Westchester. The great exodus to Connecticut had not yet begun. White Plains was the smallest of its designated cities, the biggest being Yonkers, and the others including New Rochelle and Mount Vernon. In 1935, White Plains was the northernmost urban outpost of the county. Beyond were just the villages such as Bedford Hills, Armonk, and, of course, Greenburgh, the site of Wisteria Cottage. It was a bustling little city with a raffish newspaper, the *Reporter*, and there was a great community-mindedness to it. It obviously would grow and grow, and it did. The main drag was called, logically, Main Street, and it was on this chief street that the county courthouse, some fifteen years old, sat in its comparatively majestic glory.

The trial of Albert Fish began on Monday, March 11.

HUNDREDS OF townspeople crowded around the courthouse, and some pushed and shoved their way into the trial room itself, where State Supreme Court Justice Frederick P. Close was presiding. At the prosecution table were Elbert T. Gallagher, an assistant district attorney who was to conduct the case, with an assistant, Thomas D. Scoble, while sitting with Fish at the defense table were Dempsey and an assistant, Frank J. Mahony. Fish himself made a strange sort of murder-trial defendant. In an ill-fitting gray coat and vest, with rumpled blue shirt, badly-knotted striped tie, and his gray hair and mustache freshly trimmed, he seemed so . . . so scrawny, with his moist blue eyes appearing to pop out from above his thin, slightly wattled neck. He settled himself into his seat next to Dempsey and almost immediately put his hands across his face, looking out now and then through his spread fingers—a posture he was to maintain for most of the trial.

Newsmen from all over the metropolitan area, naturally, were on hand, and Norma Abrams, the "sob sister" of the New York *News*, pulled out all the stops in her description of the old man: "A bizarre bit of shrunken humanity in whose twisted soul the savagery of primal man vies with a horde of modern vices of the worst sort."

Gallagher was a brisk and businesslike attorney (later he would become State Supreme Court Justice) who began his opening remarks calmly enough but gradually got into the swing of things and, after describing Fish's walking away from the Budd home with Grace, said solemnly, "The afternoon passed, the night went by, and she did not come back." He was feeling his thespian oats so much that Dempsey rose and objected to "the dramatics on the part of the district attorney."

Gallagher lost no time in getting down to brass tacks. He would, he said, through the testimony of medical experts, prove that Fish was sane, "that he is not defective mentally, that he has a wonderful memory for a man of his age, that he has complete orientation as to his immediate surroundings, that there is no mental deterioration, but that he *is* sexually abnormal, that he is known medically as a sex pervert or a sex psychopath, that his acts were abnormal.

"Now in the first instance," the prosecutor said, "in this case there is a presumption of sanity. This defendant is legally sane. But he is sexually abnormal. His acts were abnormal, but when he took this girl from her home on the third day of June, 1928—in doing that act and in procuring the tools with which he killed her, bringing her up here to Westchester County, and taking her up to this empty house surrounded by woods in the back of it, he knew it was wrong to do that, and he is legally sane and responsible for his acts.

"That is a brief résumé of what the people will prove in this case." Gallagher played to an attentive house. Those in the crowded courtroom, from the dozens of newsmen to judge and jurors, listened closely to the assistant district attorney's brief address. Fish seemed to be dozing, head on one hand.

Dempsey, a bit more theatrical than Gallagher, promptly established his defense. He would, he said, bring "overwhelming proof to demonstrate conclusively, beyond any doubt, that the man was insane in 1928 and is insane today." In his remarks, he referred to Fish's 1930 stay in Bellevue Hospital, pointing out that, after the old man was discharged as fit to take his place in society, Fish married three more women without benefit of divorce. "Bellevue," he said dramatically, "has a lot to account for here, I submit."

The impaneling of a jury proceeded with normal efficiency, with perhaps a few more unusual requests for being excused than usual. Seventy talesmen were examined by 5:30 P.M., and from among them, nine were chosen as jurors, the first and thus the foreman being John Partelow of Mount Pleasant, a carpenter and foreman. Many prospective jurors had to be dismissed because they said flatly they already believed Fish to be insane. Of the other reasons, one possible juror said he was getting married, and another said he couldn't leave home for any length of days because his wife couldn't tend their furnace. Meanwhile, as this dreary side of the trial went on, Fish ate a ham and egg sandwich at noontime and promptly got an upset stomach.

Most of the audience watching these flat proceedings seemed to be trimly dressed women, with several hundreds more milling about in the outside corridor, complaining bitterly about being locked out of the courtroom. Besides Partelow, the jurors picked on the first day of selecting a jury were Harry J. Cooper of Rye, retired; Walter J. Crum, Jr., of Pelham, a carpenter; Gilbert J. Nee of Yonkers, a steamship agent (a bachelor); Joseph J. Garland of Mount Pleasant, retired; Henry J. Euler of New Rochelle, an electrical engineer and also a Sunday School teacher and Scoutmaster; Clarence L. Clark of White Plains, an office manager; and Louis L. Hirsch of Scarsdale, an office manager.

Although the prosecution used six of its thirty peremptory challenges and the defense one, that first day, the jury selection went comparatively rapidly and smoothly. Dempsey asked the panelists if they ever had been treated at Bellevue or Kings County hospitals and also brought up cannibalism, asking if testimony about it would influence the juror unduly. "Some of the evidence," the defense counsel said, "may be gruesome, shocking, and brutal." He also asked the prospective jurors, in the event they should find Fish insane, "Will you agree to send him to Matteawan for the Criminally Insane?"

Gallagher, in his questions, stuck pretty much to the one issue: "If you find that Fish knew the difference between right and wrong, will you vote him guilty?"

The trial began in an atmosphere of decorum. "I'm going to conduct a quiet, orderly trial, if that is possible," Justice Close announced—obviously thinking of the wild and woolly Hauptmann trial for the kidnap-murder of the Lindbergh baby that had gone on in New Jersey. For the first time in twenty years, a Westchester jury was to be locked up each night. The nearby Roger Smith Hotel was picked as its lodging place.

When the second day of the trial began, the selection of the jury was finished promptly with the choosing of George L. Burkle, a Yonkers carpenter; William D. Foster, a New Rochelle dental supply salesman; and James Dolan, a New Rochelle restaurant proprietor. The alternate was Thomas F. Madden, a Yonkers iron worker and the only other bachelor on the panel.

The prosecution got into its case immediately. Mrs. Delia Budd, Edward Budd, Jr., and Edward Budd, Sr., were the first three witnesses called, and each of them positively identified Fish as "Frank Howard." A heavy woman in black, Delia Budd made the identification in a high, nasal voice, and, although Dempsey asked her if she hadn't identified the previous defendant Pope "with equal certainty" in 1930, Gallagher brought out that she had retracted that identification.

The senior Budd's identification of Fish had a touch of drama to it. With his bad eyesight—the cataract on one side and glass eye on the other—he had to be led by one of the dozen deputy sheriffs in the courtroom down to the defense table where Fish sat. Meanwhile, six other deputies closed in on the defendant, should there be an outburst of any kind.

As Budd shuffled toward Fish, the old man slumped into his chair. Four feet away, Budd began to peer forward. When he was a mere twelve inches from Fish, he looked intently, as a deputy put a hand under the old man's chin and propped up his face. Slowly, Budd nodded. "That's the man," he mumbled. "That's the man who took my child away." Then, after tapping Fish on the shoulder, Budd broke into deep sobs and groped his way back to the witness chair. He took a little while to recover. Looking at Attorney Gallagher, Budd shook his head. "That's enough to make anybody shiver—that sight," he said.

Aside from identifying Fish, young Budd had little to say in testimony. He did say the defendant in 1928 had fuller cheeks "and his hair has turned a little bit. The mustache is a little bigger." Mrs. Budd identified the agate pail in which Fish had brought the pot cheese to her home and said that Grace had been confirmed only a month before being taken away. Asked about the Pope identification, she simply shrugged and said, "Well, I made a mistake."

The senior Budd had only one pertinent piece of testimony to add to his identification. When Fish had come to the Budd home for that fatal, second time, he said, "I showed him where the telegram [the one Fish had sent saying he was delayed in New Jersey on business] was. It was up on the mantelpiece. He deliberately goes over and he picks the telegram up and he puts it into his pocket."

DETECTIVE KING was put onto the stand rather late in the afternoon. Carefully, methodically, he told the story of the stakeout at the East 52nd Street rooming house and how, when he asked Fish if he had written to Mrs. Budd, the old man had hesitated for several minutes and then answered, "Yes, I did."

"Were the contents of this letter the truth?" King testified he asked Fish. The old man shook his head.

"No, that wasn't the truth," he said. "I had a brother who was in the navy. When I was a little boy, he used to come home from the navy, having been assigned to duty in the Far East, and tell the stories." Fish, King said, claimed he didn't know Mrs. Budd and never had met her.

The detective then described taking Fish to the cottage, the night of the day he was arrested, and he said Fish

"seemed delighted that he was able to lead us to his secret."
Dempsey asked him if Fish had admitted cannibalism to
him, and King said no, he hadn't.

"Did he say he had read books on cannibalism?"

"Yes."

When court was resumed on Wednesday, King still was
on the stand and he went on with his story of the events immediately following the arrest. During the interrogation at
headquarters, he testified, he said he had told Fish he was
going to send for the Budds and for Willie Korman, to identify the defendant. The old man had grimaced, then sighed.
"Don't send for those people," he said finally. "I'll tell you
all about it. I'm the man you want." The confession—the
first confession—followed.

King said Fish told him that, since the murder, he had
"been up there [Wisteria Cottage] four or five times with
my son," and he added that while Fish *had* admitted reading books on cannibalism and having talked about it frequently, he would not admit that wanting to eat human
flesh was an obsession with him. The detective also identified a rambling, incoherent letter that Fish had written to
him from Eastview Jail on December 16, in which he
blamed his "woes" on his early years in the orphanage in
Washington. "Misery leads me to crime," Fish wrote. "I saw
so many boys whipped, it ruined my mind." King testified
that Fish in the orphanage "learned to lie, beg, steal and
saw a lot of things a child of seven should not see," para-
phrasing Fish's own words.

The rest of the day's testimony was routine. Frieda
Schneider, proprietor of the rooming house in which Fish
was picked up, said a "Mr. Fish" had lived there for a few
months, and she identified the old man. Sergeant Hamill's
brief testimony corroborated much of King's, and he added
that Fish had told him that he went often to burlesque

93

shows. Other prosecution witnesses were Joseph Prefer and Joseph Leary, New York police department photographers; Mrs. Marguerite Pettingill, a social worker at the Northern Dispensary in Little Falls, New York; Mrs. Mabel E. Donaldson, a dental hygienist there; and Herman L. Vielefeld, chief of the dental clinic there. Grace Budd, it seemed, had been sent to Little Falls in the summer of 1927, and their testimony dealt with the identification of the dental work on the small girl's skull found in Greenburgh.

When Gallagher had Grace Budd's bones brought into court in a cardboard box, Dempsey got to his feet and objected violently. "Never in Westchester history," the defense lawyer exclaimed, "has the skeleton of an alleged murder victim been brought into court." He moved for a mistrial—denied—and the skull was tagged Exhibit Thirteen. The other bones had similar tags.

As Dr. Wertham recalled later, "The *corpus delicti* was presented in the courtroom in a cardboard carton, and the district attorney frequently and dramatically rattled the bones both figuratively and actually. . . . An anthropologist from Johns Hopkins University, called in to identify definitely the bones of the victim, had found an acorn carefully preserved along with the bones. That acorn appeared in the cross-examination of one of the medical witnesses: 'Don't you know that among what were claimed to be human bones was an acorn?' "

Another letter written by Fish in jail to Detective King was introduced, and in it the old man had noted, "If I had not written to Mrs. Budd in November, I wouldn't be in jail now. Suppose I deny the killing. I have signed no statement yet. Had I not led you to the spot, no bones would have been found. I could be tried only for kidnaping. It was my fate for doing wrong." In the letter, Fish also described how he liked to torture himself with fire and needles, and he said

94

that he once had written to twenty widows who had advertised they had money. "All hot air," Fish's letter to King concluded. "Asking the blessing of almighty God for you, I am, Albert Fish." Forty-six other Fish letters were introduced as exhibits: They were from Fish to women, answering advertisements, and usually they contained obscene or mildly obscene suggestions—in the main that he, Fish, wanted the women to whip him.

ON THURSDAY, two of Fish's confessions were read—one to the New York assistant district attorney, Marro, and the other to Frank Coyne, the district attorney of Westchester. One of the confessions was close to two thousand words and the other ran more than double that in length but, as the court clerk droned on, Fish brightened perceptibly and seemed to enjoy the proceedings, nodding his head alertly at one passage or the other.

The lengthier confession, to Coyne, contained Fish's statement: "I kept track of the case in the papers. If they'd have accused someone else of the murder, I would have come forward. My best days are over." Coyne said he had a third confession in which the old man admitted knowing right from wrong. It was not introduced as testimony, but the way was paved for its presentation if necessary.

In the confession to Coyne, Fish was asked, "Did you have to keep hacking away to get the head off?" He replied yes. "Did you get any sex pleasure from the murder?" "No sir, no sir. No sex evidence at all. I did not outrage her."

The rest of the day was given over to bits and pieces of prosecution testimony, including further identification of the teeth in the little skull, and the statements of Frank R. Cudney of Worthington, whose mother owned Wisteria Cottage; District Attorney Coyne; and a number of Greenburgh policemen who had been engaged in digging up the bones of Grace Budd. At nightfall Dempsey held a brief session with newsmen and told them flatly there was "no doubt that Fish had practiced cannibalism." It was the first time the subject had come up directly with regard to Fish, as far as the reporters were concerned, and their major problem in learning of it was just how and what they could tell their readers about it. Dempsey also gave his opinion that Fish was a man of dual character, the one aspect gentle and religious, the other capable of atrocities.

BY FRIDAY it was time for two of the Fish children to take the stand. The first was Albert, Jr., now thirty-five, a short, balding man in a bright blue shirt, and it was under Dempsey's dogged cross-examination that he told for the first time of Fish's preoccupation with religion. "Up until September of 1934," he said, "I lived with my father at 1883 Amsterdam Avenue in New York, but long before that, in the early twenties, we lived in Greenburgh.

"In 1922, six years before Grace Budd was killed, I was playing football with my brothers—near Wisteria Cottage. I looked up and saw my father standing up on the top of a knoll. He had his right hand raised to heaven and was screaming 'I am Christ!' He walked back and forth and kept repeating it."

The junior Fish also told of having seen his father beat himself with one of two paddles he had that were padded and studded with inch-and-a-half nails. "He told me," Fish, Jr., said, " 'I use them on myself. I get certain feelings over me. When I do, I've got to torture myself.' " He also testified that, at the time of the full moon, his father had an intense desire to eat raw meat and once when Albert, Jr., found that all his father had prepared for him was a plateful of it, he said the old man told him, "That's the way I like meat and you'll have to like it that way, too." Young Fish also described how his father had built a trap and sprinkled lime on the basement floor in Amsterdam Avenue—to catch what appeared to be a nonexistent black cat.

There had been, incidentally, a full moon on the night of June 3, 1928. The New York *News* took full recognition of the fact, and in one of its headlines referred to Fish as "a moon maniac." Later Dr. Wertham was to comment dryly, "The court was asked to take judicial cognizance of the phases of the moon, for which purpose a *World Almanac* was produced in court."

Thirty-one-year-old Gertrude DeMarco followed her brother on the stand, and emotionally she told how she had lived with her father until she married. She was thirteen, she testified, when her mother walked out on Fish in January of 1917. All the children had gone to the movies in the afternoon and, she said, when they returned they found the house empty and all the furniture gone.

When Fish returned from work that night, Mrs. DeMarco said, he took the children to Mrs. Fish's sister in Flushing, Long Island, to stay for several nights, then went to White Plains for a week, and finally transported them to nearby Elmsford to live in an apartment house called the Flatiron Building. Her mother, she said, had gone away with a boarder named John Straube and later on came to Elmsford to see Fish again.

Strangely (she testified), Mrs. Fish had asked if she could bring Straube to live there with them but Fish said no—that she could stay but he could not come. Straube, Mrs. De-Marco said, came anyway, and Mrs. Fish hid him in the attic, taking him food secretly. When Fish found out, he said she still could stay but Straube would have to go, "so she left and went to New York City somewhere."

That, Fish's daughter said, was the last time her mother and father lived together. After living in the Flatiron

Building awhile, the small, motherless brood went to another apartment in Perkins Avenue, Elmsford, and finally to New York City.

She confirmed the story that Albert, Jr., had told of finding needles secreted in a book, which needles her father had admitted using on himself when "certain feelings" came over him. "When I can't stick them in myself," Fish had added, "I like to torture other people with the pins." Mrs. DeMarco also confirmed that her brother had not been over-friendly with their father and that yes, the father had been convicted of larceny at one time and sentenced to the Elmira Reformatory.

Her father, Mrs. DeMarco added, frequently was moody and would get up from the dining table and eat his meal later by himself. She said that he said grace at every meal, attended church "most of the time," and read the Bible frequently. She didn't remember his ever having struck any of his children or having talked harshly to them.

Gallagher then read to the jury some of the letters Fish had written to his daughter from jail in January and February, showing his bitterness toward his wife and Albert, Jr., and Fish at this point buried his face in his hands and wept, while Mrs. DeMarco, too, sobbed on the witness stand. She finally was so overcome that Gallagher excused her from the stand, and he finished reading the letters without her there.

The final witness for the state was Dr. Roy D. Ducksworth, an X-ray specialist at Grasslands Hospital, and he seemed a rather odd prosecution witness in that he carefully, methodically described the several dozen needles in Fish's body and identified the X-ray photographs of them. When the state rested, Dempsey made the expected move to dismiss the indictment, and he asked for a directed verdict of insanity, both of which Justice Close refused.

IT WAS A cold, windy pre-spring weekend in White Plains, and the jurors remained in custody at the Roger Smith, mostly playing pinochle or bridge or reading. Under guard they were taken to the movies several times and for automobile rides, while some attended church services. Back in Eastview Prison, Fish chatted amiably with his jailers and every so often fell on his knees for long periods of prayer. The outside world went on as usual. In Germany, Hitler tore up the Versailles Treaty and ordered a conscript army of five hundred thousand men. Alexis Mdivani and Barbara Hutton agreed to divorce—"the finest man I know" and "the most marvelous girl"—after twenty-one months of marriage, and Doris Duke was in Wardha, India, discussing the machine age with Mohandas K. Gandhi.

> He is a man of splendid abilities, but
> utterly corrupt. He shines and stinks
> like rotten mackerel by moonlight.
>
> —John Randolph

9. AS THE SECOND week of the trial began, Defense Attorney Dempsey made a switch in plans: He decided not to put the old man on the witness stand, possibly because he had so many lucid moments in his conversations. "Would you put that man on the stand?" Dempsey candidly asked the army of reporters covering the trial. "You would not. He admits he killed Grace Budd, but I'm not willing to accept the state's *corpus delicti*. I'm going to fight that all the way through." In view of the extensive identifications of the dental work on Grace's skull, it appeared that Mr. Dempsey was, in this respect at least, doomed to a losing fight.

Dempsey began his defense campaign with a reading of some of Fish's letters. First there were letters to his children. To John: "If you had not joined the C.C.C., I would not have been here. I intended to carry my story to the grave. I had no money, no money. Love, your poor old daddy." To Henry: "Winter is going. Spring soon will be here. And the birds will come. Good times are coming. Love, papa."

Then there were the obscene letters Fish had written to various women. Two of the women, Mrs. Grace E. Shaw and Mrs. Helen Karlsen, testified in court as to the sending and receiving of the letters and, during the reading of them, Justice Close twice cleared the courtroom of women. Mrs. Shaw, who lived in Little Neck on Long Island, said she had turned Fish's letters over to postal authorities and, indeed, had kept up a correspondence with Fish to enable the government men to try to track the old man down. Most of the letters to her from Fish, as read in court, harped over and over again on his desire to have himself—variously "Jimmy Pell" and "Robert E. Hayden" (who wanted Mrs. Shaw to care for his insane son, Bobby)—whipped and beaten.

In replying to these, Mrs. Shaw testified, she wrote, "Mr. Pell, there is no reason why I should have to whip you. There is no need for it. You are not a patient of mine. Were I to do such a thing and you dropped dead, I would be held for murder." She added that Fish—whom she identified positively—had come to her Long Island home with a rope, and she also said that in his very second note to her, he had proposed marriage.

Mrs. Karlsen had an even closer relationship with the old man. In 1927, Fish and two of his sons, Albert, Jr., and Eugene, came to live with Mrs. Karlsen, a Brooklyn widow, and she said that during this brief period, she got three obscene letters from him, all placed under the door of her room. One of them said Fish was going to a lodge meeting and expected to be tarred and feathered; he would give her forty dollars to remove the mess when he returned.

Fish's sons left the house for good before he did, Mrs. Karlsen continued, and she reported that she once "bunked into him" in a hallway when "he was standing there in his union suit." Finally, frightened and disgusted, "I told him he would have to get out," and after he left she found a nail-studded paddle in his rooms. Also, Mrs. Karlsen said shyly, "He left a little mess around the room when he left. I don't like to say what it was."

Dempsey pursued the one course in his defense and he put everyone possible on the stand to prove the old man's legal insanity. There were, this day, four of his children, a grandchild, and a seventeen-year-old stepdaughter by a bigamous marriage, and each of them testified to actions by Fish that were eccentric to say the least.

The seventeen-year-old was Mary Nicholas, the Bartlett, Ohio, girl to whom Fish had written the strange letter of birthday congratulations from jail—the one that ended with the unrelated news that anyone with a quarter could go into the West Side "Y" and see a couple of hundred naked men and boys swimming. Mary was one of seven children of Mrs. Myra Nicholas and, looking almost solemn behind a pair of glasses, she testified that Fish had visited her widowed mother for a week in January of 1929, had married Mrs. Nicholas—and then had vanished after another week. It was, of course, just one of the several bigamous marriages Fish entered into after the Grace Budd slaying.

"My two brothers, my little sister, and I used to play with him," Mary said. "He would go to his room every night and come back wearing only a pair of brown trunks. Then he would play a guessing game he called 'Buck, buck, how many hands up?'

"He gave us a stick and, when we didn't guess right, we'd beat him with the stick. He'd tell us to hit him harder. We also played a game called 'sack of potatoes,' during which we would slide down his back, clawing him.

"Every night after we would get through playing the

games, why he would go to the toilet and he took all the paper off the roll and lit it, and he had a big fire. My mother would tell us to put it out and he looked kind of mad about it. He done that every night."

The Fish children added more fuel to the defense. John Fish, twenty-four, wearing his drab Civilian Conservation Corps uniform in court, described how, when he and his brothers Albert and Eugene were living with the old man in Long Island City in 1925 and 1926, his father was in obvious pain during one breakfast time, and said only, "Well, last night I stuck a needle into myself." John also said Fish told his sons that his real name was Hamilton—that he had had a younger brother who had died at childbirth and that he, Fish, had taken the infant's name of Albert.

Henry F. Fish, the old man's youngest son—he was twenty-one now—described how his father had for three days poured oatmeal into several holes on the porch of their home in Astoria, Long Island, without any explanation.

Mrs. Anna Collins, thirty-four, Fish's oldest daughter, said that her father had behaved very strangely during the days they lived in Elmsford. One early morning about two o'clock, she said, she went downstairs from her bedroom and saw Fish rolled up in a carpet in the foyer—where she found him, still there, the next morning. "He says St. John the Apostle told him to sleep there," Mrs. Collins said. She added that her father had come to live with her and her husband in September of 1925, staying until the spring of 1928, when, Fish told her, "God told me to leave." The old man returned in November of 1928, had a hernia operation, and then left for good.

Little Gloria DeMarco, eleven, had a simple addition to the defense testimony. She said that several times she had seen her grandfather "hitting himself with a stick."

On Tuesday, Dempsey put twenty-seven-year-old Eugene

Fish on the stand. The son repeated the story of the football game in Greenburgh, when the old man had stood on a hilltop and cried out that he was Christ, and he added that in 1927, when he was helping his father in a job at the Royal Palm Apartments in Brooklyn, he saw Fish standing nude in front of a window—painting a window casing . . . with a dry brush.

The defense testimony took another bizarre twist after young Fish's testimony. A New York City detective named John P. Smith told of the events in 1930 that preceded Fish's arrest and detention in the psychiatric ward at Bellevue Hospital.

Smith said the department got a telephone call from the proprietor of a Long Island boarding school, whereupon he was sent to an address in Rockaway Beach, where he found that Fish had been living while working as a dishwasher-porter-handyman. The woman manager of the hotel took Smith to Fish's room, and there the detective found an old matrimonial journal, a ten- or twelve-week-old frankfurter in a drawer, a carrot, and a small cat o' nine tails. After this discovery, the witness said, Fish was taken to Kings County Hospital in Brooklyn and, after an examination of a week or two, discharged as reasonably harmless.

It was shortly thereafter that, chiefly following up the correspondence between Mrs. Shaw and Fish, using his Pell and Hayden aliases, postal authorities arrested him for sending indecent literature through the mails. Fish was taken to Bellevue in mid-December of 1930.

> The sick are the greatest danger for the healthy; it is not from the strongest that harm comes to the strong, but from the weakest.
>
> —Nietzsche

10. BELLEVUE HOSPITAL'S psychiatric ward, now so overcrowded, even then was too full of patients for any detailed examination of any single one. Under the direction of Dr. Gregory, the staff seemingly did the best it could—but the best was none too good, especially when the patient involved was a man such as Fish. . . . warped sexually and God knows in how many other ways, but still passably sharp and keen of intelligence.

On December 18, 1930, he was given his first "full" examination, and the over-all summation of him was: "Average intelligence, with inability to adapt to unfamiliar material."

There seemed little doubt that Fish had pulled out all the stops in trying to present a "normal" human being to the Bellevue examiner. He was marked in this fashion on this report:

105

Cooperation: full.

Attitude toward situation: self-reliant.

Attitude toward examiner: friendly.

Attitude toward test material: spontaneous.

Type of response: reflective.

Attention: sustained, on the whole.

Emotion: average.

Motor control: average.

Responses: precise, generally.

Emotional response: variable.

Remarks: considerable unevenness in test performance, which is due to unevenness of abilities rather than to emotional factors.

One of the aspects of this particular test was a vocabulary question involving some fifty words. Fish got most of the definitions right, but this was how he messed up on the few that he didn't get:

Artless: "personal opinion regarding art."

Harpy: "a sort of personal opinion."

Retroactive: "falling back on the one who contemplates to do wrong."

Perfunctory: "puffed-up manner in official."

Piscatorial: "refers to scenery."

Fish also failed to get the definitions of the words ambergris, achromatic, sudorific, and shagreen—but then, not many people would have.

The Bellevue report concluded that Fish showed:

"Prompt, satisfactory social contact; good verbal facility in spontaneous productions; adjusts rather smoothly to controlled test material; satisfactory attentional control; memory functions on the whole well preserved; prefers verbal to concrete tasks; tends to recur to discussion of his difficulties, but returns to tests of his accord; occasionally shows signs of resentment, but appears capable of adequate emotional control."

From that evaluation, at least, it would have been an exceptional psychiatrist who could have deduced that the man described was a cannibalistic murderer.

On December 23, 1930, Fish was questioned in detail again, this time by Dr. Gregory's immediate assistant, Dr. LaGuardia. He told the psychiatrist that he had started writing obscene letters after "reading a bunch of letters a chauffeur found in a garage at Dr. Robert Lamb's Sanitarium in Harlem." The old man said he had been a painter there and that ten years before that time, he wouldn't have written such letters, but "this was a pretty tough bunch of fellows up there in Harlem. At night, we were all in one room, playing cards, reading, and writing letters. I just guess I got into the habit of writing those letters."

"Before that," he was asked, "you never had any desire for anything of this sort?"

"No sir, not at all."

"As a painter, you must have heard a lot of smutty stories."

"Yes. I have traveled a good deal in different states. You hear different stories in different ways."

"How did you react to these stories?"

"Sometimes I would listen and sometimes I wouldn't. I never drink."

"You read these letters which you found at the sanitarium?"

"Yes."

"Why didn't you disregard them, just like you did the stories?"

"I got a letter from a young girl and she was very frank and that kind of started it going."

"How did you come to meet her?"

"She was formerly a waitress at Dr. Lamb's."

"How did she happen to write you?"

"She came up there a couple of times while I was a painter there. She had gotten into some trouble with a man and they were both discharged. She came up there afterwards to see one of the young fellows she knew and that's how I came to meet her."

"Was it just a mere acquaintance?"

"That's all."

"Why should she write this letter to you?"

"Probably she was trying to incite me in that way, because that's why she was discharged."

"What happened after that?"

"I don't know what happened to her. When I got into that first trouble, I was acquainted with an elderly woman, seventy-one years old. We had been corresponding and were engaged to be married. I wrote her and she engaged Mr. I. F. Goldenhall and paid him three hundred and fifty dollars to defend me. When I got arrested this last time, I wrote to him and he said that he had spoken to United States Attorney Carlson and that if I wanted him to defend me, I should raise some money."

Getting back to the letters Fish wrote, Dr. LaGuardia asked him how he had felt when he wrote them.

"I had no particular feeling," the old man replied.

"Did you feel that you *had* to write these letters?"

"It was just sort of a habit."

"Would you dream about these things?"

"No sir."

"Did you think about them?"

"No, they are not in my mind at all."

"Did you read books and magazines on it?"

"No, sir. Those clippings I had were given to me."

Then, for no apparent reason, Fish went into a small biography of himself, touching on his married life. "I am supposed to be a widower," he volunteered, "but I am not. My

108

wife is the mother of three illegitimate children besides my six. We were living at 1013 Fifth Avenue, College Point, in 1917. I was at White Plains at the time. I used to stay up there because it was too long a trip to come twice a day. She went to Harrison Street, Bridgeport, Connecticut, with this fellow. His name is Straub. He was a boarder in our house. They lived as man and wife. They came back to College Point. She is still living. My children know about it."

The questioner asked him how he had felt about his wife "running away with another man."

"I took it very hard," Fish said. "It hurt me very much. She sent me word that, if I let her bring those two illegitimate children to my home, she would come as my housekeeper, and I never answered her letter."

"Is it true that people put advertisements in the newspapers saying they wanted housework, and you would answer them by writing obscene letters?"

"No."

"That's the charge against you."

"I can prove it. I have letters from the woman who made the charge."

"This colored girl in Newark who brought charges against you—you sent her obscene letters in answer to an advertisement?"

"No, that's not true. She wrote me a letter. That case was thrown out. I had the letter to prove it."

"You mean, in no case did you make the first advance?"

"No. In every case, I got a letter written to me."

"You kept on writing these letters, didn't you?"

"After I got into trouble, I never intended to let them know what the charge was."

"How could you prevent it?"

"Unless someone told them of it, they wouldn't know."

"Why did you write these letters, if they didn't give you pleasure?"

"I couldn't give any definite reason for it. I just got into the habit of writing them."

"When was the last time you had intercourse?"

"Two years ago."

"Have you had any desire since that time?"

"No."

The "them" that Fish referred to, when saying he didn't intend to let on what the charge against him was, apparently meant his children, although he didn't elaborate on it and the questioner didn't press the issue.

As for the clippings found on him when he was picked up by the postal authorities, they included one dated Chicago, dealing with the marriage of two nudist couples; one dated Berlin, about three hundred and twenty-five persons having been voluntarily sterilized; one from Hamden, Connecticut, about nudists found bathing, and one out of Lille, France, dealing with the "transfer" of a female into a male through an operation.

Dr. Gregory digested the various reports made by his aides at Bellevue and then wrote to Judge Frank J. Coleman of United States District Court that Fish was "abnormal—a psychopathic personality with evidence of early senile change, but not insane or a mental defective."

Such a change, Dr. Gregory went on, was not uncommon in men of his age. The psychiatrist told Judge Coleman that Fish was "quiet and cooperative, orderly and normal, with no evidence of delusional notions or hallucinatory experiences." He added that the old man showed signs of "sexual psychopathy [sex perversion], which happens to men of his age but is not significant here because Fish has manifested sex perversion from early life." The old man's only physical liabilities, he concluded, were arteriosclerosis and a mild nephrotic disorder.

After the Bellevue report was received by the court, Fish

was discharged from the hospital as sane and put on six months' probation.

WHEN DR. FREDRIC WERTHAM took the stand on that Tuesday, March 19, Dempsey questioned him only briefly. He preferred to let the eminent psychiatrist tell his findings in his own way. Which, with a minimum of cross-examination by the prosecution, he did.

He had, the doctor began, had long, detailed sessions with Fish on February 12, 15, and 25 and had uncovered at least a rough history of the old man and his family. Fish told him, he said, that he had had a brother die at eighteen of "water on the brain." That, Dr. Wertham said, "medically meant syphilis."

Fish's father—"who called Albert a 'stick in the mud' "—died when the boy was five and when the child was sent to the orphanage in Washington, he apparently was the youngest boy there. At the orphanage, the inmates "committed all sorts of sensory acts with each other, in which he joined." Fish had told him, Dr. Wertham said, that one of the "guardians"—evidently a sister or teacher—had whipped the boys frequently . . . stripping six at a time and belaboring them while the others watched. The old man told the psychiatrist that he had gotten his "first sex feeling" during these episodes. Fish also added that he had wet the bed until he was eleven.

Fish's sex career, Dr. Wertham opined, began when he was about seventeen, "and I believe, to the best of my knowledge, that he has at least raped one hundred children." The old man's prime interest, he went on, was children from the ages of five to fourteen or sixteen. "Or, he was afflicted with paedophilia."

All through Fish's life, so far as he could ascertain, the psychiatrist stated, "women were just a substitute." He was

111

basically a homosexual. In his young manhood, according to the story Fish told Dr. Wertham, he traveled in Europe and "went to Brussels and practiced oral perversions on the rectums of men and women and so on. He was extremely interested in urine." He evidently practiced as a homosexual prostitute at that time, and when he visited the famous Eden Musee in London he got the idea of castrating boys, from having viewed "some anatomical things."

When Dr. Wertham described "the Kedden episode," Justice Close once again ordered the women in the courtroom to withdraw.

Kedden had been a youth who had "bummed his way" into St. Louis from the west or south on a banana train. He was a nineteen-year-old who looked three or four years younger and, the psychiatrist declared, must have been defective.

"Fish met the boy, picked him up, and took him to his room in St. Louis, giving him money and clothes," Dr. Wertham testified. "He forced this boy to urinate on him. He whipped him. He cut him a little bit—the way he expressed it. He had this man whip him and he played all sorts of games. One was the father and one was the child, one was the teacher and one was the child. And he forced him to do all these things to him, too.

"Eventually, at the last moment, he arranged it so that this boy would get an erection, and while he had that, he took a knife and cut part of it off." The psychiatrist said Fish also told him he had cut the youth's buttocks with a razor blade and attempted to drink his blood.

"He intended also to kill him," Dr. Wertham said, "but he told me that he saw the look on this boy's face and he couldn't stand it, so he left a ten-dollar bill—and he left the city." He said that Fish reported this as happening about twenty-five years before, but added that the old man was rather unreliable about dates.

112

Dr. Wertham proceeded with his grisly tale.

"He has on a number of occasions taken flowers, taken roses, and he inserted these roses into his penis, or he inserted them into his rectum, and then he would stand before the mirror and look at himself," the psychiatrist said. "He would get sexual gratification from that. In the end, he would eat the roses."

Fish had married when he was in his thirties and his wife was nineteen, Dr. Wertham said. "He made sure before he married her that she was interested at least to some extent in some of the things he was doing," he said, "and his relations with her were entirely abnormal."

The old man told him that he had read all he could obtain on violence and torture "and used it for masturbation purposes. He liked very much to expose his nude body," Dr. Wertham said. "He also had an enormous desire to do the opposite again—namely, seeing other people nude."

The stories that Fish told Dr. Wertham conflicted here and there—as the psychiatrist admitted candidly—but his sessions with the old man had been so long and thorough that, "The way in which he told me these things—I mean, I can only tell you, it rang true. It seemed to me those things were true and I believed them." What Fish stated, he continued, "might be fancies, but I have never seen fancies which showed on an X-ray," referring, of course, to the several dozen needles discovered in the defendant's body.

Again—fact or fancy? "He makes a clear distinction between that—he makes a clear distinction between what he really did and what he intended to do."

Getting down to the specifics of the Grace Budd episode, Dr. Wertham told the court Fish admitted to him that he had told police things that "were not true." He quoted the old man: "I told them down there that I took my clothes off because I didn't want to get her blood on me. Doctor, that is not true. I took my clothes off just for pleasure, the actual reason."

Dr. Wertham then made the first flat statement about Fish's cannibalism. "He definitely told me," the psychiatrist testified calmly, "that he ate the flesh of Grace Budd."

While the old man was on his way home after the murder—carrying parts of Grace's breast and abdomen—"he was picturing what he was going to do, and he had a sexual discharge on the way home, carrying it."

It took him nine days to eat the parts of Grace. "I asked him how it tasted," Dr. Wertham said, "and he said it tasted like veal, and he told me he prepared it with carrots and onions and gravy, and that for nine days he lived in an absolute state of excitement, sexual excitement, about this matter." The old man, Dr. Wertham said, ate the flesh during the day and masturbated at night.

Dr. Wertham then took a long, professional look at the facts he had uncovered.

"I can tell you that to the best of my medical knowledge," he stated, "every sexual abnormality that I have ever heard of, this man has practiced. Not only has he thought about it, not only has he daydreamed about it, but he has practiced them. He has shown the most, I might say, incredible cruelty that one can think of."

After a brief recess, Dr. Wertham continued his testimony, and discussed Fish's preoccupation with urine. "For a child," he said, "it is perfectly normal to play with his urine, because he does not know what that is. For an adult, it is exceedingly abnormal. His psychosexual development is in many respects on that of the level of a child, roughly speaking."

He gave his professional opinion that "from the strife of his mind, this is not the only murder he has committed." He then testified that it was his belief, based on his long analyses of Fish, that the old man had, over a fifty-year period, attacked at least a hundred children in twenty-three states.

Dr. Wertham quoted Fish again: "What I did must have been right, or an angel would have stopped me, just as the angel stopped Abraham in the Bible."

The Fish children, sons and daughters, were, of course, in court all during Dr. Wertham's testimony, and they obviously were in deepest despair, particularly Eugene, who had been in tears when he had been on the stand telling of his father's self-torture. During the brief recess in Dr. Wertham's appearance, Edward Budd was introduced to Mrs. DeMarco in the corridor outside the courtroom, and he told her gently, "There's no hard feelings. You had nothing to do with him. I'm not blaming you."

The young woman had tears down her cheeks. "We're all so dreadfully sorry," she said.

Dempsey was finishing up the preparation of a fifteen-thousand-word hypothetical question dealing with the sanity or insanity of a defendant such as Fish, but meanwhile, before his introduction of it—that would be on the following day—he couldn't resist asking Dr. Wertham for an off-the-cuff opinion about the defendant.

"He does not know the character and quality of his acts," the psychiatrist said. "He does *not* know right from wrong. He is insane now and was insane before." He then elaborated a bit, saying that Fish was not idiotic or stupid. "His thinking processes are not affected," Dr. Wertham said, "which is true of the vast majority of insane people."

THE NEXT DAY, Dempsey, after having stayed up most of the night with his associates, working, introduced his fifteen-thousand-word hypothetical question, covering forty-five typed pages, dealing with all of the strange and bizarre acts Fish was accused of, and leading up to the final simple query: In the light of all this, do you consider the defendant to be sane or insane? However, before he got a chance to start reading it to Dr. Wertham, Gallagher objected that he hadn't had a chance to read it, so for two hours or so, he, Dempsey, and Judge Close were in chambers, studying the hypothetical question and making minor changes in it. At 11:12 A.M., Dempsey began reading it to the psychiatrist, and an hour and twenty-five minutes later he had finished. He put the sheaf of paper to one side and looked at the witness. "Assuming that all these facts are true," the defense counsel said dramatically, "can you state whether or not in your opinion, Albert Howard Fish is sane or insane?"

"I can," Dr. Wertham said calmly. "He is insane, a victim of mental disease."

He elaborated a trifle. "Fish suffers from paranoiac psychosis number three," he went on, "—or, a psychopathic personality and an organic change of mind, possibly caused by arteriosclerosis of the aorta." The medical jargon seemed to irritate Judge Close, and he addressed himself to Dempsey. "Did he mean that Fish did not know right from wrong?" he asked. Dr. Wertham turned to him.

"I mean just that," he said. "He had a perverted, insane knowledge of right and wrong."

YEARS LATER, in his *The Show of Violence*, in one chapter of which he dealt with the Fish case, Dr. Wertham went into a fuller explanation of his diagnosis and also commented on his testimony in general. "What is a psychopathic personality?" the psychiatrist asked.

"A psychopathic personality is a vague term which means a mild kind of abnormality not gross enough to be called a mental disease, but which, on the other hand, does not permit one to call a man who has it completely normal. Many

116

patients who are not mentally diseased, not insane, are therefore classified in a vague general way as psychopathic personality—which means only that they have an abnormal mental makeup. I gave it as my opinion that, quite apart from the later developing paranoid psychosis, Fish's mental makeup was so abnormal that on that alone, according to the mental hygiene law, one could and should have committed him long since to a civil state hospital. None of the facts that I stated, including the cannibalism, were contested, but my opinion about his legal insanity was challenged."

He entered a mild defense for the art of psychiatry, which, he said, "is by no means as vague a science as some who do not know it, or who practice it unscientifically, like to assume.

"There are many well-established data. For example, a patient will not talk about his delusions right off, or about his hallucinations either. Frequently they have to be elicited by careful, prolonged examination. Paranoid psychoses frequently remain unrecognized and undetected for a long time until a complete and competent psychiatric examination is carried out, based on subjective and objective data. Coprophagia is *always* an indication of mental disease, and cannibalism in our time, with the exception of extreme catastrophic hunger situations with impending death, is unthinkable for any person in his right mind. In psychiatric hospitals and in mental hygiene clinics it is customary to commit to state hospitals those individuals whose mental state is such that they are a danger to themselves or others."

GALLAGHER HAD kept after Dr. Wertham almost relentlessly on the knowledge-of-right-and-wrong question but had not shaken the psychiatrist from his convictions. Finally Wertham stepped from the stand and Dempsey replaced him with another psychiatrist, Dr. Henry A. Riley. Dr. Riley agreed with Dr. Wertham and added a few items of possible explanation. For one, he said, Fish had been hurt in a fall from a tree when he was eight and had had headaches and dizzy spells ever since, and for another, he said the defendant had suffered sunstroke in the past and also may have had his nervous system affected by "lead colic," the painters' occupational disease.

"He [Fish] told me that there were frequent occasions when he would have visions or what he called visitations, in which he would see the face of Christ or the whole body of Christ, garbed in various kinds of raiment, showing the marks of the nails in the hands and the feet," Dr. Riley testified, "and often said that he could see blood actually coming out of the side of Christ. And usually when the visitations occurred, that he could see the lips of Christ moving and that he would be saying things to him, giving him definite messages.

"I believe this delusional state is still existing with him and I therefore believe he is not sane."

Under cross-examination by Gallagher, Dr. Riley said Fish told him he had tried to drink some of Grace Budd's blood, but that after the second or third mouthful he had become nauseated and had vomited. Then, under re-direct, the psychiatrist refuted the possibility that the old man had been faking his seeming insanity or hallucinations. "A man cannot manufacture a psychosis any more than he can manufacture an attack of typhoid fever," Dr. Riley said. The doctor's credentials, incidentally, were in high order: He was professor of neurology and psychology at Columbia University's College of Physicians and Surgeons.

Late in the afternoon, in his testimony, Dr. Riley said that the month before at Eastview Prison, Fish had told him he had a "direct command from God to sacrifice a virgin." At this point Clarence Clark, juror number eight, interrupted the testimony to ask Riley if a man could be a religious fanatic and yet succumb to physical passion. Dr. Riley rubbed his head and nodded. "Yes," he said, "that's perfectly possible."

Dempsey then put Dr. Smith Ely Jelliffe, a neurologist who was not unfamiliar with murder trials—long years before he had testified at the trial of Thaw for the slaying of White—on the stand. Dr. Jelliffe said that, during his pretrial examinations of Fish, "I picked up a lot of little holes in his mental apparatus, clearly indicative of some deterioration and disorganization."

Dr. Jelliffe apparently had been confided in to a great extent by Fish in the matter of Kedden, the young man he had picked up in 1925 from the "banana train." Before leaving the train and going with Fish, the youth had been in the company of five Negroes on the train for days and they "carried on almost all kinds of sexual activities, consisting mostly of fellatio and homosexuality."

"The man was covered with lice," Dr. Jeliffe said. "He [Fish] got a patent hair remover such as the ladies use and stripped all the hair off the other's body, including the hair off his pubis—and then for a period of two to three weeks or more, they carried on all kinds of mutual sadistic and masochistic sexual perversions and activities."

It was during this sordid episode, the psychiatrist declared, that "Fish began going into trances for five and six days and he really wouldn't come out of it until he had finished either these masochistic or sadistic activities with orgasm." Dr. Jelliffe added his opinion that the old man apparently had gone into "a partial trancelike state until after Grace Budd was dead," and said Fish had had two emissions during the killing of the little girl.

All the world is queer save me and thee; and sometimes I think thee is a little queer.

—Unidentified Quaker to his wife

11. THE STATE, of course, had its own experts to testify to Fish's sanity or insanity, and Dr. Wertham later described their appearances on the witness stand as comprising "one of those legal battles of experts so often said to give a black eye to psychiatry." The doctor added, with seeming rue, that this wouldn't be so "if the eyes of official psychiatry—and especially forensic psychiatry—were not already bloodshot."

Certainly the state's experts made Dr. Wertham lose some of his heretofore impressive objectivity. He dealt with them later in this almost cavalier fashion: "One of them was professionally associated with a district attorney's office. Another was a regular psychiatric adviser to the district attorney of the county. One was the chief of both of the public psychiatric hospitals where Fish had been 'observed' some two years after the Budd (and other) murders—while he was still being sought 'high and low' on that account by the police!—and there declared both harmless and sane.

"All four agreed on the diagnosis of psychopathic personality, which one of them amplified by adding that 'I should say that the proportion of those who walk the streets who are psychopathic personalities is at least 25 percent, if not more.' Two of these psychiatrists based their testimony on one joint interview they had with Fish one evening. One of them became so agitated and excited on cross-examination that the court had to declare a recess until he could collect himself enough to allow the trial to proceed."

In brief, Dr. Wertham didn't think a great deal of Gallagher's experts. Nonetheless:

The four were Dr. Menas S. Gregory, former head of the psychiatric division at Bellevue Hospital; Dr. Perry M. Lichtenstein, medical assistant to the New York District Attorney; Dr. James F. Vavasour, former chief psychiatrist at Grasslands Hospital in Westchester; and Dr. Charles Lambert.

Dr. Gregory, visibly nervous, testified that eleven psychiatrists had examined Fish at Bellevue between December 15, 1930, and January 5, 1931, and that they had been under his personal direction. There were, he added, few records of the old man's stay there because ultimately he had been found sane and therefore no thorough examination of his background had been kept. He took up the matter of the assorted perversions that had been charged to Fish.

"It's a common sort of thing, these perversions of Fish," Dr. Gregory said. And when Dempsey, cross-examining, asked him if he "would consider a man who does such things as all right," he replied:

"Not perfectly all right, but socially all right. There are men high up socially and financially who unfortunately suffer that way. They know right from wrong. They are successful people."

Dempsey—almost scornfully—grilled Dr. Gregory about

the methods used to examine patients at Bellevue, and when he insinuated that Fish's examinations had been done in a slipshod manner, Dr. Gregory half rose from his chair and almost yelled, "In a city hospital, you know, we have to do the best we can!" Dempsey nodded. "And often that is none too good?" he suggested. "It's very excellent," the psychiatrist said. Dempsey lingered a moment on the fact that one of the Bellevue reports said Fish had been found praying in a bathtub, and Dr. Gregory said there wasn't anything indicative in that. "I suppose that was the best place he could do it," he said, "because the rooms were so crowded with other patients."

Dr. Lichtenstein's testimony was a little less emotional. Discussing his examination of Fish, he said the old man told him of one episode in 1918, when he was living in the Bronx. Fish went to see a widow who had advertised furniture for sale and later made several other visits to her. He influenced the woman to come and live with him, with her eleven-year-old daughter, and one day when the little girl was ill and home from school, the widow went to the store and "Fish approached the child, played with the breasts of the child, played with her sexual parts, and then exposed himself to that child. I asked him why he did that. He said the reason he did that was because it gave him a certain thrill, a sexual feeling, that it satisfied him sexually."

Dr. Lichtenstein said Fish told him he worked frequently in churches because, "Well, I like the choir boys," which tied in with Dr. Wertham's belief that the old man basically leaned toward homosexuality, and he said that, when Fish was at St. Ann's Church in the Bronx as a sexton, he liked to watch the boys take showers.

"He made the acquaintance of two boys in particular," the witness said, "and he said they were plump lads and had them come up to his room, and he said that these boys would undress and that they would have sexual relations with one another, and that they would have sexual relations with him, and that he would have relations with them, practicing sodomy."

Dr. Lichtenstein's testimony in a way just seemed to add to Dr. Wertham's monumental list of Fish's perverted ways —but then, when Gallagher read a thirty-six-hundred-word hypothetical question (only a fifth as long as Dempsey's but cut to the same pattern) Lichtenstein said flatly, "The defendant was sane." He added that Fish three times had asked him, "Doctor, can't I be found insane?"

Dr. Lambert, following Lichtenstein on the stand, testified that Fish told him he had "played with her [Grace Budd]. I handled her breasts. I fingered her between the legs. I took her up on my knees and spanked her." The psychiatrist said he had asked the old man if he dreamed.

"I have had many nightmares," Fish allegedly replied. "I wake up frightened. Sometimes I wake up thinking that Grace Budd is back and I reach out to get her and she is not there." Dr. Lambert added, however, that as far as he could ascertain, Fish never fainted, never heard "voices" and never really was "under any unnatural influences."

Defense counsel Dempsey questioned Lambert about the fires that Fish supposedly set on toilet floors. "Would that," he asked, "indicate to you that there was any mental disturbance in the man's mind?" Dr. Lambert shook his head.

"No," he said. "I construed that it was a form of sexual stimulation."

When he testified that it was his belief Fish "has a psychopathic personality—without the psychosis," Lambert was picked up quickly by Dempsey. "Will you state that that man could for nine days eat that flesh and still not have a psychosis and not have any mental disease?" he shot at the psychiatrist.

123

"Well," Dr. Lambert replied, "there is no accounting for taste, Mr. Dempsey."

Lambert said that he supposed it appeared almost absurd to say Fish was sane despite his cannibalism, but that he still could be defined thus by the law. "We run into extraordinary things," he added. Dempsey then asked him if he knew of any other persons who actually ate human feces.

"Oh," Dr. Lambert said, "I know individuals prominent in society—one individual in particular, that we all know."

"That actually *ate* human feces?"

"That used it as a side dish with salad."

Dr. Vavasour, the fourth prosecution psychiatrist witness, said Fish told him that, after the birth of his third child, he "reverted to the practice of contacting boys and girls." Apparently, he said, the old man had then "had" about twenty-five to thirty boys and girls "and hundreds of sessions." He referred to the Bronx widow with the eleven-year-old daughter. "The child slept with the man and this woman," Dr. Vavasour said, "was able to see their acts and, with the permission of the woman, the acts were practiced on the child." Summing up, he gave his opinion that Fish represented "a deviation from the normal in his adjustment toward life, toward the usual average things of life as we know them."

"In other words," Dempsey said, cross-examining, "he is a mental case?"

"I did not say that. What do you mean by 'a mental case'?"

"In your opinion, doctor," Dempsey said, "can a man drink urine and eat human feces and not have a psychosis?"

"He can," Dr. Vavasour replied.

The state rested its case at 4:45 P.M. on Thursday, March 21. Just before Judge Close adjourned court for the day, Fish passed a scribbled note over to Dempsey. "Before you sum up," it said, "read to the jury Isaiah, chapter 26, 12th verse, and Jeremiah, chapter 19, 9th verse. Have Mary see me." It was the most cryptic of notes. The verses cited refer to some of the consequences of sins of Jews as predicted by the major prophets. And "Have Mary see me." Mary Nicholas? There was no further explanation from the old man.

ACTUALLY, CONSIDERING the shock and luridness of so much of the trial, the summations by both defense and prosecution counsel were a little disappointing. Dempsey's was impassioned, as expected, and Gallagher's was more or less factual—but somehow, neither struck off any sparks. It was as if the compact, sometimes almost unbelievable, vagaries of the trial itself had worn down the two lawyers and they were almost just going through the motions.

Each took about two hours that Friday. Dempsey told the jury that, when police finally solved the Grace Budd murder case and came up with the old man, "they found a maniac." "Mr. Gallagher," Dempsey said, "will tell you this crime was planned, was deliberated on.

"All animals plan. The fact that a man can connive and plan an outrageous, dastardly, fiendish crime like this is no indication of the fact that a man is in his right mind." In trying to sketch the manner in which a man can kill without it having any bearing on his intelligence, the defense counsel drew on his own World War One experience, when in basic training he was taught to use a bayonet. It resulted in one of the very few moments of levity in the trial. Getting to his feet, Gallagher seemed to have a twinkle in his eye as he made a mild protest.

"I just wish to note here, your honor," he said, "that I want the privilege of speaking about my naval service."

Judge Close smiled. "I think we might concede here," he said almost benignly, "that you two gentlemen won the war."

In his summation, Dempsey explained why he had not put the old man on the stand. "I do not believe an insane man should be on the witness stand, testifying," he said. "Secondly . . . the story of this man's life is one of unspeakable horror. You wouldn't believe it; it would disgust and nauseate you."

Finally, he appeared to have abandoned completely his side issue of questioning the authenticity of the box of bones as the *corpus delicti*. "The only question to be decided here, gentlemen, is what will be done with this man," Dempsey said. "That is all." He summed up his opinion of his client: "A Jekyll and Hyde personality, a homicidal maniac for at least fifty years, until 1928—when everything snapped."

Gallagher's summing-up, which took about the same two-hour stretch that Dempsey's did, was more or less factual, calmly delivered—and, as expected, dwelt heavily on the belief, buttressed by the four prosecution analysts' opinions, that Fish knew right from wrong.

"If this defendant were operating under psychosis," the prosecutor reasoned, "how could he tell you all of the details about the killing of this girl?" A point well taken, of course, and yet at odds with Dr. Wertham's thesis that a psychosis had nothing to do with a man's intelligence, and that many "insane" persons were sharp and clever but still off-balance.

"I will admit," Gallagher added, "that he [Fish] engaged in revolting practices with women and children and others. But the law does not say that, in and of itself, allows him to commit murder with impunity against the innocence of childhood." The "innocence of childhood" phrase was one of Gallagher's few melodramatic statements.

DR. WERTHAM listened to the summations, particularly the prosecution's, with head-shaking and a depressed feeling. He was thinking of some of the statements made by the prosecution psychiatrists under oath:

"The family background of a patient is not always necessary. If I am insane, then my family history might help me—but if I am not sick, it is not necessary."

"Danger has nothing to do with the commitment of mental cases."

"Paranoid individuals are usually rather frank and free and let things out rather easily."

"It is a matter of appetite and intensive satisfaction, and the individual may do very repulsive things and still be a seer; I mean, a very wise man."

"I have not seen any cases laboring for years under a psychosis without it being ascertained."

"In his psychosis, there would not be any lucid intervals. He either has it or he hasn't it."

"One finds within about half an hour that the patient has paranoia."

"If a man takes alcohol and puts it on cotton and puts that into his person and sets fire to it, that is not masochistic; he is only punishing himself and getting sex gratification that way."

And perhaps the most extraordinary comment—Wertham used the word "extraordinary" in his *The Show of Violence* to describe all these statements—was the one referring to "picqueur acts," a phrase he himself had brought up during his testimony. This is a technical term referring to the habit of sticking needles or other sharp objects into oneself or others—and yet one of the experts said that yes, he knew all about it, that a picqueur "is one who peeks, and peeking doesn't mean a thing."

Judge Close's charge to the jury took an hour and eight minutes, during which he pointed out to the panel that it had seven choices of verdict. Then he discharged Madden, the alternate juror, and newsmen buzzed after Madden and drew from him the comment that he personally felt Fish was insane. And finally, during the judge's charge, the cluster of reporters took a poll among themselves and concluded that the old man was legally insane.

The jury got the case, then, at 3:01 P.M. on Friday, March 22. It deliberated almost four hours, with time out for a 6 to 7:30 P.M. dinner at the Roger Smith hotel, and filed back into the old courthouse at 8:28 P.M. to hand up its verdict.

Guilty. The death penalty was mandatory.

THE OLD MAN'S face was uncovered—one of the few times during the trial that he had not sat with face buried in his hands—and his facial muscles seemed to contract and contort. He had to be brought before the bar to hear the sentence and he didn't seem able to stand, so two deputy sheriffs lifted him from his chair by the elbows and almost carried him to face Judge Close. There in a low, mumbling voice, he said he was sixty-four, a Protestant, a temperate man who had been educated in public schools, whose address was 75 East 128th Street, New York, and that he had a criminal record.

As the reporters rushed out to hunt for available telephones, Close went over to the jurors—who among them had twenty-four children—and shook the hand of each, after Court Clerk George Ellrodt had polled them individually. Some of the newsmen stopped by the defense table and asked Dempsey what he thought of the verdict. He shook his head.

"The man is insane," the tired lawyer said, looking up. "Even among perverts, he was an incredible person. I can't understand—I just can't understand—how twelve intelligent men could have decided he was sane." Then he nodded slowly and said yes, he would appeal.

Five of Fish's children were in court, this final day—although Albert, Jr., had been in the corridor as the jury deliberated and the doors were shut in his face when he tried to return—and of them, only Eugene showed any immediate real emotion; tears filled his eyes. Fish's two daughters, however, had delayed reactions and had to be helped from the courthouse. Edward Budd, Jr., had been in court, and he said simply to the newsmen, "It was what he deserved."

Fish? Once he heard the verdict, he looked chagrined. "I feel bad," he said. "I expected Matteawan." But then his other side—or one of his other sides—came to the fore. He almost smiled.

"What a thrill that will be," he said, "if I have to die in the electric chair. It will be the supreme thrill—the only one I haven't tried." Then, contrite again: "But it wasn't the right verdict. I'm not really sane, you know. And my poor children . . . what will they do without me to guide them?"

Before being returned to Eastview Prison, Fish spoke briefly to Dempsey in Sheriff Thomas F. Reynolds' office on the first floor of the courthouse building. "How did my family take it?" he asked. "They were scattered about the courtroom and I didn't have a chance to talk with them." He peered at the lawyer. "Will you come up to see me in the jail?" he asked, and Dempsey assured him he would.

In the Budd apartment, back in New York, there seemed general elation. The ailing, half-blind senior Budd said that, when he heard the verdict, he had "a funny feeling. It hit the top of my head when I realized he would go to the electric chair," he said slowly. "It put a tremor through me. But he deserved it. Insanity was the bunk."

Mrs. Budd again was brief and to the point. "Just what I expected," she said with obvious relish. "Good for him!"

Fish's sentencing, a technicality, was set for Monday; it

merely remained for Judge Close to set a date for his electrocution in the chair at Sing Sing. Court slowly began to clear out. The old man was put into a van and taken back to Eastview. The people, as the saying goes, had spoken.

Man-like it is to fall into sin,
Fiend-like it is to dwell therein—.

—F. Von Logan

12.

OVER THE weekend, Fish never was alone. There always was a guard outside his cell. The state wanted to be sure it had a defendant at the moment of sentencing Monday morning. However, the old man showed no signs of wanting to harm himself. On the contrary, he was almost affable—as he signed a statement confessing to the murder in 1927 of Billy Gaffney, the four-year-old Brooklyn boy who had vanished on February 11 of that year and not been seen since.

Warden Casey at Eastview said Fish had admitted the Gaffney murder voluntarily during a half-hour talk—but the "confession" cut little ice with Gallagher or District Attorney Walter Ferris, who figured with some logic that Fish merely was trying to strengthen his chances of having the verdict overturned on appeal.

"No matter what he confesses," Ferris said that Sunday afternoon, "he is still going to be sentenced tomorrow morning. If he's still alive." Ferris said there would be no attempt to question Fish at length about the Gaffney case, since that would fall under the jurisdiction of the New York missing persons bureau.

Came Monday and the old man, in dark trousers, gray jacket, and a white-bearded stubble, stood by silently as Dempsey first tried some last-minute legal maneuvers—he made seven separate motions for a new trial and moved to have the original verdict set aside on four counts, all of which Justice Close turned down—and then Fish was sentenced.

Afterward, before he was taken to the "big house" at Sing Sing, Fish "confessed" to New York authorities that he had committed at least four other murders. One was the Gaffney case: The old man said he had killed little Billy in a public dump near Riker Avenue in Astoria, Queens, and had cut up the small body and sunk it in Bowery Bay in four potato sacks. He also said he had strangled five-year-old Francis McDonnell and buried him in a shallow grave near his home in Fort Richmond, Long Island, in 1934. He had planned to cut up the McDonnell boy, too, Fish said, but a passing milkman frightened him out of that.

Then there were other, relatively vague crimes. Fish said he "probably" killed a man in Wilmington, Delaware, in 1910, and that likely he had mutilated and tortured to death a half-wit in 1919 and a Negro boy on a houseboat in Georgetown, District of Columbia.

There was no reason, of course, that he could not have been telling the truth—yet his dates were so confused and there was such a cloudy air to the "confessions" that the general attitude of questioning authorities was that the admissions were not true. And for another thing, Wilmington authorities wired to New York that there was no case on record of a mutiliated half-wit, while Inspector Frank W.

132

Burke of the Washington, D.C., detective force, who supervised the Georgetown area in 1919, said there was no record of a Negro boy's having been stabbed as Fish had claimed.

In another section of Superior Court in the White Plains courthouse, young Lawrence Stone, who had pleaded guilty to second-degree murder in the death of Nancy Jean Costigan of Mount Vernon, was sentenced to from fifty years to life. Stone, the ex-convict and alleged mental defective who had made life so miserable in Eastview for Fish with his profanity, was almost jolly as he was led away to a room where Fish waited. The mustachioed Stone was manacled to the old man—"Isn't it bizarre," one newsman pointed out, "that both of these men are descended from Revolutionary families and indeed, that Stone's ancestors have been in Connecticut for two hundred years?"—and they were transported to Sing Sing. There, Fish became convict number 90,272 and Stone number 90,273.

THE EXECUTION was ordered for the week of April 29 but, quite naturally, no one expected it to take place then because of the appeals. Dempsey took the case first to the Appellate Division and then on to the Court of Appeals, losing both times. The attorney still found it hard to believe that a man such as Fish, whom he so firmly believed to be insane, would be sentenced to death.

"Albert H. Fish's insanity," he said after the Court of Appeals turned down his plea, "was disregarded by the jury, undoubtedly through passion and prejudice.

"His conviction proves merely that we still burn witches in America."

Dempsey was busy elsewhere, too. For one thing he got every one of the jurors in the case to sign an appeal for executive clemency. For another, he visited Fish frequently in Sing Sing, and it was there that the old man repeated his story of having killed others. "Who and where?" the attorney asked. "There's a body in the Riker Avenue dump in New York City," Fish told him.

Dempsey and a friend went to the dump on a Sunday, but it was a needle-in-a-haystack venture. There were all kinds of bones, from dog skeletons to roast-beef leftovers. The area was so huge that there just was no logical place to begin a search. Returning in several days to Sing Sing, Dempsey told Fish, "You've got to give me a better location" and the old man finally sketched out an area where he thought the body—that of a boy from Staten Island—would be. Dempsey returned to the Riker Avenue dumping ground once more and hunted, but with no luck.

The months dragged on and at last a rather firm date of execution was set, for January 16. Dempsey made a final visit to the death house in Sing Sing before his last legal effort—a hearing before Governor Herbert Lehman to try to win executive clemency—and he reported that "Fish talked to me about all his sexual and religious ideas and gave me documents so obscene that I couldn't show them to anybody."

ALBANY, New York State's capital city, is a hundred and forty miles north of New York City, a seedy sort of city, with old, run-down houses, an air of yesterday about it— and winter weather comparable with Canada's. The Capitol Building, an ornate stone structure with all sorts of stairways, entrances, and exits, sits atop a long hill of a street that stretches through the business district of the city, and it has a cold, almost forbidding look, like something out of a Hitchcock movie. It was there, on one of the chilliest of January days, that Lawyer Dempsey gathered his forces for the final time and tried to save his monstrous client from the electric chair. Gallagher and others from the Westchester

District Attorney's staff were there, Dempsey and several associates, and Fish's two daughters and three of his sons. Finally, the gathering included Dr. Wertham, who, like Dempsey, found it hard to believe an insane man was going to be electrocuted.

Dempsey and Gallagher started off before an impassive Governor Lehman, by virtually renewing their White Plains court battle. Dempsey asked immediately for commutation of the death sentence and urged that Fish be confined in a state institution for the criminally insane.

"When the case was argued before the Court of Appeals," Dempsey pointed out, "the chief judge remarked 'there is no doubt that this man is insane, but the question is, does he come within the legal definition of insanity?'" The defense counsel leaned forward toward the governor. "You, Your Excellency," he said, "are not bound by the legal definitions of insanity."

Gallagher more or less contented himself with stating that the death penalty should be carried out as ordered. "This is one case," he said, "in which I cannot see one single fact that deserves leniency on your part."

Dr. Wertham's comments were by far the longest of the session, and they were impassioned, although the psychiatrist delivered them with neat orderliness to make his point. He began by standing before the governor and outlining the case more or less briefly. "No more concrete objective evidence of a man's mental abnormality could possibly be demonstrated than the X-rays in this case," he said, referring to the photographic plates that showed the location of the several dozen needles in the old man's body.

"I am not appealing," Dr. Wertham went on, "on behalf of Mr. Fish—who doesn't mind the electric chair anyway, in his distorted ideas of atonement. He is, in my opinion, a man not only incurable and unreformable—but also unpunishable.

135

"I am appealing on behalf of his many child victims. I am appealing also on account of the many victims, past and future, of such men as Fish. Most of his victims, if not all of them, belonged to the poorer classes of the population. Many of them were Negroes. All of them were unprotected by the present setup.

"Years ago this man could have—and *should* have—been confined permanently in a state hospital for mental diseases. Why, in the two months preceding his trial, I myself made out commitment papers for more than one hundred and sixty patients without any court hearing. And many of them were not so sick as Albert Fish, and none of them so dangerous."

As he warmed to his topic, Wertham was watched by Governor Lehman, but the distinguished statesman-politician gave no hint of his feelings. He had a legal aide sitting at his left hand, and the aide seemed to be approving of most of what the psychiatrist said. He frequently nodded as if in agreement. He smiled at times, and at other times he seemed seriously moved by what was being said. He, not Lehman, gave Wertham encouragement to continue.

"If you uphold the judgment of sanity implicit in the death sentence of this obviously ill man," Dr. Wertham said, "you uphold officially the policy of psychiatrists who on two different occasions have had under observation a man who had butchered and eaten more than one little child more than two years before, and who have the temerity to declare now that such a man was not a suitable case for commitment to an institution for the insane.

"Assume what might easily have been possible: through some technicality, say a doubt about the identity of the *corpus delicti*, had existed and this case had to be dropped legally. Are you as a statesman telling me as a psychiatrist that I have no right to commit this man to an institution for the insane? And that the community has to wait until he has tortured and killed still another child—and been caught—before it can safeguard itself?

"The choice before you is whether you want to endorse abstruse psychiatric sophistries or the efforts of those who want to see that the children of the community will be protected in the future."

Dr. Wertham went on to explain that beyond a doubt he considered Fish a sick man and "to execute a sick man is like burning witches. The time will come when the psychiatrists will be as little proud of their role in these procedures as the theologians are of their role in the past."

Science, he continued, "is prediction." The science of psychiatry is advanced enough that with proper examination such a man as Fish can be detected and confined *before* the perpetration of these outrages, instead of inflicting extreme penalties afterward." He pointed out: "The authorities had this man, but the records show that they paid no attention.

"A man who practices cannibalism under these circumstances has a deranged mind. I have spent more time examining this man than all the prosecution psychiatrists combined. If he is electrocuted as sane, then you—to whose personal conscience the law entrusts this case at the moment—will give your stamp of approval to all the callousness and unconcern of those whose duty it was to protect the children of the community."

Dr. Wertham—upset by the impassive mien of Governor Lehman and not knowing really whether he should continue or stop talking—said to the state executive that he was not appealing to him as an expert, "because if you had all the facts assembled, including the other murders committed by this defendant, and their circumstances, you would not need an expert.

137

"I am not appealing to you for clemency," the psychiatrist said, almost heatedly now. "I am appealing to you as a statesman. In this case all the hair-splitting about legal definitions was just a covering up of a social default. I am asking you to commute the death sentence to lifelong detention in an institution for the criminal insane—and to make this case an example and a starting point for a real scrutiny not of individuals nor individual institutions, but of the whole haphazard and bureaucratic chaos of the psychiatric prevention of violent crimes."

Later, Dr. Wertham was to say that on that occasion, before Governor Lehman, "I had had an image of an occasion where the very law specified that a high authority had to sit in his capacity as a human being, using his personal judgment to listen and decide. That was an old tradition that used to be jealously guarded by emperors and kings. These rulers on such occasions rose above the feudal lords and their vassals. I felt that this was the opportunity for once to reach the ear of a human being in authority.

"But I didn't succeed."

Nor did he. Wertham was the final speaker of the afternoon. When he was done, Governor Lehman got up from his chair slowly, made a half nod and then, followed by his aide, left the room. There was to be no executive clemency.

THE DATE of execution was January 16, 1936. All day, Warden Lewis Lawes of Sing Sing stayed near a telephone, in case Governor Lehman should call to stay the electrocution, but there was no call. A newsman asked the warden how he felt about the legal killing of such a man as Fish. Lawes merely replied, "I am not supposed to feel. I am just part of the apparatus."

The customary complement of reporters and official witnesses was on hand when the old man came into the death chamber—walking even a bit more briskly, it seemed, than usual. He appeared totally calm and self-possessed. Indeed, he didn't even appear to be elated or excited at the thought of the new thrill he was going to experience. He walked to the electric chair, seated himself, and even helped attendants fix the electrodes to his legs. Just before this, incidentally, he handed one of the defense lawyers several sheets of paper on which he had written in a scrawled handwriting.

"I shall never show it to anyone," the lawyer told reporters later. "It was the most filthy string of obscenities that I have ever read."

The switch was thrown, finally, and the oldest man ever to be electrocuted at Sing Sing was sent on his way—but not quite. The first charge of electricity didn't seem to do the trick. Clouds of smoke seemed to swirl around Fish's head. Ted Worner, a prominent New York City publicist in later life, who then was a young reporter for the Yonkers, N. Y., *Statesman,* was among the spectators, and he said that apparently the dozens of needles in Fish's body had in some way caused a minor short circuit. "They gave him another charge," Worner said, "and it worked and he was dead— and with a number of others, I went outside and retched."

There was the usual autopsy, and it was found that all of Fish's vital organs were in normal condition, except for diverticulosis of the colon.

The old man was gone.

13.

SO THE old man was dead. Had justice triumphed, as the tabloids used to headline their Sunday supplement stories? Or, again, what was justice in this case?

We reach back over thirty-five years and we find that Albert Fish:

Beat himself with a nail-studded paddle.

Inserted more than two dozen needles into his body over a period of years.

Slept now and then rolled up in a rug, which he said had been a religious command.

Stood on a hilltop and screamed, "I am Christ!" while his young sons played football below.

Practiced cannibalism—seemingly obviously more than just the one time with little Grace Budd.

Started fires on bathroom floors with rolls of toilet tissue.

Ate raw meat when a full moon was out.

Drank urine, ate human feces, and at least once tried to swallow human blood.

140

Tried to kill himself in his jail cell with a sharpened chicken bone.

Sprinkled lime on a basement floor to trap a nonexistent black cat.

Had nineteen known perversions, or nearly a dozen more than any previously known case.

Married in 1898 and at least three times more without benefit of divorce.

Was described by his daughter, six years before his electrocution, as mentally ill.

Was in and out of mental wards in hospitals, as he was with police stations.

Had a family history of feeble-mindedness.

Admittedly had—the admissions from both prosecution and defense witnesses—a "paranoid psychosis."

Wrote endless obscene letters, such as the one in 1929 (listed in the Bellevue report) to a Mrs. Ralston, in which he said his "dickey belongs to you" and "you and your tail to me." In which he said he would strip and spank her behind —her "big, fat, sweet behind," which he would "eat up," and "We will do it in every way." And the one to Mrs. Shaw in 1934 when he wrote, "I shall drink quarts of your sweet No. 1 and eat pounds of your sweet No. 2."

ALL THIS, THEN—all this and not insane?

Not *senile dementia*, to be sure; old age had little to do with a career begun in the teens. Not the syphilitic *dementia paralytich*. Hardly *encephalitis*. But a *traumatic psychosis*, possibly, or *dementia praecox?* Mustn't there be some medical term, somewhere, somehow, that fit Albert Fish? More easily, for instance, than any term applicable to normal people, whoever they may be?

Justice Close and the prosecution laid down a simple criterion, which indeed may have been pretty much the law of the land in those nineteen thirties: Did the man know right from wrong?

Can this simple rule-of-thumb test settle so easily the issue of whether a man is insane or not? Dr. Wertham testified, with what objectively seems detached logic, that many insane persons know right from wrong. Many of them kill, maim, or torture with the full knowledge that what they are doing is against the law of nature—but they cannot stop themselves from doing it. Or, as seventeen-year-old William Heirens of Chicago wrote in lipstick on a wall after he had committed a brutal slaying: "For heavens sake catch me before I kill more I cannot control myself."

D. L. CHAMPION, in his *The Sexual Psychopath*, wrote of the old man: "There is no doubt that Albert Fish was one of the most maniacal sadomasochists that ever lived. But it is a curious thing that no matter how depraved a man, no matter to what his iniquities may descend, there always remains in his subconscious mind some vestige of the virtuous homilies he learned at his mother's knee. Albert Fish was insane in every aspect of the word except the one that mattered most to him. Legally, he would be adjudged as rational as a computer. He had committed murder. He had indulged in every perversion mankind has invented. He was helpless when in the grip of the terrible sexual urge that descended upon him from time to time. Nevertheless, there was something buried deep inside him that was still able to recognize evil, still able to discriminate right from wrong."

Champion quoted Dr. Richard H. Hoffman, a well-known New York psychiatrist, on this drive, this urge:

"Hunger will make a man kill to eat. It will make him eat his own shoes. When that hunger is sexual, a similar drive controls conduct. Any obstacle will be destroyed. A deer chasing a doe during the rutting season will attack even a bear if it's in his way. Sex is governed by visceral, primitive urges which destroy all insight, deliberation and inhibition."

The public at large, of course—and this takes in virtually any twelve-man jury that must put its feeling into law—is wholly uneasy with this kind of thing. Its simplistic outlook usually—and unfortunately, according to such experts as Dr. Wertham—takes the form of, well, he knew exactly what he was doing, so he is as guilty as hell. A jury after deliberating six hours came in with such a finding in the case of Albert DeSalvo, the Boston strangler who killed thirteen women in a year and a half (and gave him a life sentence that could see him eligible for parole in twenty-six years). The clean-cut, all-American boy Heirens was sentenced to "an imprisonment from which he shall never return." There are dozens of such cases, and only now and then one such as Winnie Ruth Judd's, she being the infamous "trunk murderer" of the early thirties who was branded mad by a sanity board and committed to an Arizona asylum (from which she escaped seven times).

THE JURORS in such cases—or even 98 percent of the public when you put it to them—come up with the old argument, "Well, suppose Grace Budd had been *your* daughter?" The question is almost irrelevant. It's in the same category as the deep Southerner's, "Well, would you want your sister to *marry* one?" Laws are not made by people who have been scarred or deeply hurt by the violent and the mad. They are made by those who can look broadly at the issue and decide what should be done, without bringing in a personal angle.

The testimony in the murder trial of Albert Fish now is in a thick, yellowing volume of more than a thousand pages stored in the basement of the old courthouse in Westchester—and if you go through it page by page, line by line, brushing away the legal maneuvers and the foolish little details with no relevance, it is difficult to see how Fish could be called sane. Knowing right from wrong seems almost incidental. The man's spiritual and mental make-up was as warped as an old tennis racquet left for years outside a press. His world was his own and its scale of values completely different from the one in which most of us exist. Yes, the old man seems to be saying through it all, it was a terrible thing to do—but wasn't it, at the same time, wonderful? Sane?

FEW MEDICAL men have gone so thoroughly into the subjects of violence and mental aberrations as Dr. Wertham and, as he has admitted freely, a psychopathic personality is a vague term meaning a mild kind of abnormality "not gross enough to be called a mental disease, but which, on the other hand, does not permit one to call a man who has it completely normal." Fish's mental make-up, he says, "was so abnormal that on that alone, according to the mental hygiene law, one could and should have committed him long since to a civil state hospital."

In researching the relationship of psychiatry to the law, Dr. Wertham found that it was the Greeks who first were cognizant of the difference between medical disease and mental disease. "When they described in their legends and tragedies the most archaic crimes of humanity, such as matricide, patricide, filicide, or cannibalism," he adds, "they skillfully introduced a shadow of madness. It hovers over the legendary figures of Orestes, Oedipus, Medea, Heracles, Thyestes."

It was around 1780 that Jean Paul Marat, a physician and politician in France, brought out a volume called *Plan de la Legislation Criminelle,* in which he made a suggestion "which is still far from being fulfilled today," according to

144

Dr. Wertham. Marat said that, in *all* cases involving sexual abnormality, the defendants should not be treated as criminals but, rather, should be given institutional psychiatric treatment. However, even in those days the prosecutors evidently were not prone to give in too easily to this theory. Wertham cites a case in Hamburg in 1805 when a clergyman killed his wife and four children. Several doctors said he was undoubtedly mad—but a philosopher (and seemingly the philosophers in those days were, roughly, the psychiatrists for the prosecution) said that in his opinion the murderer was motivated by religious fanaticism . . . and the clergyman was, as customary in those years, broken on the wheel. On the other hand, a man named Hadfield in 1800 took a shot at King George III in the Drury Lane Theatre in London, and at his trial it was determined that he suffered from a chronic psychosis with delusions of persecution—and he was acquitted and confined in an institution. So, a hundred and thirty years before Albert Fish was brought to the bar, the same problem seemed to be confronting the public.

The "Did he know the difference between right and wrong?" law that was applied in the Fish case, too, apparently has longstanding roots. In 1843, ninety years earlier, England adopted "the McNaughton rule," which defined insanity for legal purposes as "lack of knowledge of the nature and quality of the fact and of the difference between right and wrong." Within several decades, the same yardstick was adopted by American courts and, to more or less degree, it appears to have remained.

Dr. Wertham begs to differ. "Not to distinguish in criminal jurisprudence between a well man and a sick man," he says, "is like the primitive error of not distinguishing in murder cases between accident and design. Society's defense against the sick man in all stages of the procedures con-

145

cerning him must be different from those concerning a well man. That is where psychiatry comes in."

The psychiatrist, he continues, is really the only one concerned who can come up with certain facts pertinent in a criminal case where the defendant may not be a well man. The thoroughgoing psychiatrist, Dr. Wertham declares, is not there just to give an opinion; he also reveals facts that only he is privy to because of his scientific techniques. On the other hand, his is not merely a one-sided view. "The ultra-radical proposal" to turn over most or all such offenders to psychiatry "is not only impracticable, but harmful, for it deflects our attention from the present-day abuses of psychiatric criminology and from the fight against them."

THE PUBLIC'S opinion in murders with a psychiatric angle, Dr. Wertham feels, "does not always express its own best interest." Getting in the way of justice, he says, is the undeniable fact that almost everyone, from juror through editor through newspaper reader, is involved emotionally in such cases.

"Subconsciously," the doctor continues, "recognizing in himself similar impulses, he wants the man to be treated like someone very different from himself. He may want the murderer declared totally insane—and so totally different from himself and most people. In that event the murderer may go completely free with, in addition, what amounts practically to a hunting license to commit further crimes without punishment. Or, on the basis of the same kind of emotional reasoning, the public may wish for revenge and want the man declared sane and ready for the stake."

Delving further into murder, Dr. Wertham notes that primitive souls often thought of a killer as "possessed by a supernatural demon," and even today may still be looked upon in an obscure mystical way, as an exceptional being.

"People forget that the social circumstances leading to and surrounding murder in your own society are often far more impenetrable," he points out in *The Show of Violence*. To get to the core of these circumstances, a tough, hard job, is the work of the psychiatrist who, he points out, "must know not only what is permissible and what is forbidden now, at the present time, but also what was right and wrong in former times."

Almost wistfully, Dr. Wertham says that, as society moves along and gets a better idea of psychiatry and psychoanalysis, "the formal legal test of personal responsibility in psychiatric cases functions less and less well." He points to a ruling by Supreme Court Justice Benjamin Cardozo, who declared that "the mental health and the true capacity of the criminal" were all-important, as in the best spirit of the law. "When it becomes the written law," Wertham adds, "the proof of mental disorder—regardless of degree—will more and more supplement and replace the isolated test of personal responsibility."

BUT THAT is in the future—in time to come. In the nineteen thirties, as today, the law of the land was the old right-from-wrong business and, when twisted, unsavory, repulsive old Albert Fish was tried by his peers, his sociological background, his environment, his warped views of the world and people around him went for naught. He knew right from wrong and his peers (although, incidentally, they pledged to one another not to disclose anything of their deliberations) sent him to Sing Sing, carrying his old Bible, and from there to the iron maiden that was the electric chair.

THIRTY-FIVE YEARS LATER

THERE IS an atmosphere that somehow reminds you of Mr. Tutt, Arthur Train's fictional attorney, in Jim Dempsey's law offices in White Plains. There is a homeyness, an informality, almost a kind of cracker-barrel feeling. A stuffed lizard sits dustily in a corner. There is a violin case propped against a wall and, of all things, a small tree growing from a huge pot in another corner. The room is cluttered, crowded. There are a big maroon leather sofa and leather chairs and, as if some bright secretary had tried vainly to do a little modernizing, a thick tan rug on the floor that looks a little as if it were in need of combing. This is Dempsey's main office in the suite on Main Street, and through the window one can see the now-old courthouse just across the street from which Albert Fish was delivered to Sing Sing. Dempsey himself, still slim and wiry, still a busy practitioner, no longer young and, as Saroyan put it, with his hard heels hitting the sidewalk, but eyes bright with an inborn love of life and the living, sits in a chair behind the crowded desk and does a little remembering.

"When he was at Eastview before the trial," the lawyer

muses, "I went to see him often and I would at first bring a secretary with me to take notes. That didn't last long. She begged out, saying she couldn't listen to 'any more of that terrible stuff.'"

Dempsey grins and shakes his head slowly. "There just isn't any question he was insane," he said. "No question at all.

"He was mild, soft-spoken, meek—the *most* harmless-looking man. He knew all the books of the Bible. I really believe he had these visual and audible hallucinations, messages from Christ which he frankly said he didn't understand.

"Oh, he was as strange as they come," the attorney goes on. "If you check back, you'll see that he came into the courthouse for the trial in the oldest of clothes. He wasn't supposed to. I bought him all new clothes and, when he showed up in the old ones, I asked him where the new ones were. 'I flushed them down the toilet,' Fish told me."

He smiles again. "You know how Grace Budd's bones were collected in a cardboard box for introduction as an exhibit at the trial? Well, they showed up again that fall when we went to the Court of Appeals in Albany. I'll never forget that. We were there from two in the afternoon until six in the evening, and finally Chief Justice J. C. Crane rapped his gavel to end things—whereupon Gallagher said, 'What do I do with the body?'

" 'What!' Justice Crane exclaimed. 'You have the *corpus delicti* here?'

" 'Mr. Dempsey subpoenaed it,' Gallagher said—and so I had, although at the appeal I just never got around to using it."

Dempsey swings around in his chair and looks out at the peaceful surroundings of the old courthouse. It is summer of 1970 and trees are green, people are moving slowly, street noises seem muted and muffled by the heat of the day.

149

"Fish admitted to me that he had violated Grace Budd and ate her," he says. "He said he ate her and that her meat tasted like veal. I asked him if he ate all of her, and he seemed shocked and said, 'Oh, you can't eat the gristle, the ears and the nose.'

"The last time I saw him, I remember, was a week or ten days before the execution. He passed over to me some scrawled pages which he said were 'the story of my life,' thinking I might be able to sell it to one of the newspapers, and I made a couple of efforts in that direction but the papers said it was too revolting and wouldn't touch it. Fish expected executive clemency, you know. He must have been terribly surprised when Lehman didn't grant it."

Dempsey lapses into momentary silence. Then he looks up. "You know, I got a letter from him *after* he was put to death. It must have been held up in the mail a day or two. I remember what it said: 'If I were your father and you were my son, you could not have done more for me. I don't wish to die. God has more work for me to do. I should never have written that letter. Hoping you have many more cases but none so difficult as mine, sincerely, Albert Fish.' "

Dempsey gets up and walks a few steps this way and that behind the cluttered desk. "I felt so strongly about that case," he says slowly, "and even now, so many years later, I still do. Not that Fish was all that important—but recognition of this form of degeneracy and sickness might have spared others, women and children, in the years to follow."

Across the street in the musty courthouse, the usual complement of attorneys, hangers-on, judges and justices, shysters and politicians are crowded into the several floors. In an upstairs office, Elbert Gallagher, now a State Supreme Court Justice, almost a physical counterpart of Dempsey—fit and slim and bright of eye, with white tufts of hair at the side—also remembers the Fish trial.

"Oh, Jim Dempsey and I have been friends for a long, long time now," Gallagher says, "and now and then we still chuckle over Justice Close's willingness, during our summations, to concede that Jim and I won World War One single-handed.

"But we each of us, I suppose, felt just as strongly about the viewpoint we followed. If the case were to come up today, would I prosecute the same way? I would. It was, and is, my firm belief that Fish knew right from wrong, which was after all the basic issue of the trial. Oh, I conceded his abnormalities, his perversions, but they didn't cloud the other thing. He knew what he was doing and he knew it was wrong. Of that I'm sure."

IN THE three and a half decades since the old man was put to death, the case has come up for discussion countless times and often has been referred to in books and articles. For instance, when David Dressler, the former executive director of the New York State Division of Parole, wrote his book *Parole Chief* in 1952, he stated:

"It did those children and their parents no good that, after the killing, Fish was electrocuted. He should have been permanently hospitalized long before—and could have been.

"Properly diagnosing the truly insane is much easier than putting a finger on another type of violent aggressor—the psychopath, of whom there are legion. Psychopaths look and act like normal beings but they have a deep well of violence inside them. They explode unpredictably and horribly.

"They are not insane in the medical sense and cannot be hospitalized, despite the fact they may commit some of our most atrocious offenses. The startling fact is that society has made no provision for such people, erected no institutions

151

for their care. If they have not committed a crime, they can't even be locked up. They roam and kill." Dressler added that he recommended "midway institutions, half hospital, half custodial, where highly unstable individuals, whether or not they had committed crimes, could be sent for treatment, not to be released unless certified cured."

THERE IS no doubt that the Fish case left a deep mark on Dr. Wertham, the psychiatrist, who went on from those White Plains days to become one of the most noted men in his field. He still has his offices in New York City but he has a home in Bucks County, Pennsylvania, and it was there that he reached back and remembered the Fish trial—and darkly discussed its later effects on American society.

"As far as I can see," Dr. Wertham said, "that case was the first indication of a new trend in life in this country, which could be summed up as a callousness toward real violence."

This indifference toward violence of all kinds since 1935 has been of extreme concern to Wertham, and he has referred to it often in his lectures, papers, and books. It is, he insisted, a total reality. "Nobody cares," he said sadly. "If Fish were being tried today, people would care less than then."

In one paper, for instance, written in 1937, Dr. Wertham scored the movies' preoccupation with violence. "My studies of violence," he wrote, "have led me to the conclusion that human violence is not inevitable; that it is not a biological instinct like sex or the desire for good; that it is not ineradicable from human nature or from society; and that it can be greatly reduced and even eventually abolished. This is not a hope; it is a prognosis."

He referred to a statement by a state mental health director advocating that children be allowed to explode fireworks because it would "release tensions and produce a cathartic effect." Dr. Wertham pointed to an editorial in the *Journal of the American Medical Association*, with which he agreed, characterizing this as folly.

"One of the most notorious sex criminals in American history, Albert Fish, who over a period of years killed some fifteen children and violated or mutilated about a hundred others, collected sadistic literature and clippings," Dr. Wertham stated. "That did not help him, as the glib phrase goes, to get rid of his aggressions, but gave him further impetus and suggestions."

Wertham makes no qualifications when he says Fish's murder victims numbered at least fifteen. "That figure," he said, "was verified many times to me by police officials in later years." In Wertham's *The Show of Violence*, he stated that two years after the execution "a member of Fish's family" came to see him, being unemployed and trying to get a job. "I asked him how many children he thought Fish had killed," Wertham said, "and he looked me straight in the eyes and answered: 'You know, doctor, there were plenty of old, abandoned places. He'd always prowl around. It's hard to tell how many he killed.' " Even at that time, Wertham says, only several years removed from the electrocution, "one of the detectives told me he had murdered at least eight; a judge of the Supreme Court told me he had been reliably informed that Fish was implicated in fifteen child murders."

The psychiatrist shrugged. "Of course, I always have thought there were political overtones to the prosecution's side of the trial. Several of the psychiatrists they brought in were more or less regularly employed by the district attorney; if they wanted other jobs, they went along with the D.A."

Dr. Wertham shook his head, tiredly, almost resignedly. "No," he said, "if Fish were being tried today, people would care less than then."